Dangerous Peace

New Rivalry in World Politics

Alpo M. Rusi

WestviewPress

A Division of HarperCollins*Publishers*

D
860
R87
1997

Copyright © 1997 by Westview Press, A Division of HarperCollins Publishers, Inc.

Published in 1997 in the United States of America by Westview Press, 5500 Central Avenue, Boulder, Colorado 80301-2877, and in the United Kingdom by Westview Press, 12 Hid's Copse Road, Cumnor Hill, Oxford OX2 9JJ

Library of Congress Cataloging-in-Publication Data
Rusi, Alpo
  Dangerous peace : new rivalry in world politics / Alpo M. Rusi.
    p.   cm.
  Includes bibliographical references and index.
  ISBN 0-8133-2258-8
  1. World politics—1989–   2. Geopolitics. I. Title.
D860.R87   1997
909.82'9—dc21   97-13206
                                                                           CIP

The paper used in this publication meets the requirements of the American National Standard for Permanence of Paper for Printed Library Materials Z39.48-1984.

10   9   8   7   6   5   4   3   2   1

Dangerous Peace

To my son, Arto

Contents

Preface

This volume is the second in a series concerning change in the international system. The first volume, *After the Cold War: Europe's New Political Architecture*, was published in 1991. It was drafted in New York in 1989 and finalized in Helsinki in 1990. When I began my work, strategic studies and military aspects dominated the research field. I quickly recognized that a broader, more "dynamic" approach was needed to cope with ongoing revolutionary changes in world politics. There was no longer any real threat of a hegemonic war, yet the bipolar system was collapsing. The question was, what did this phenomenon contain? Instead of answering this question at the time, I could only discuss the most immediate political repercussions of the end of the Cold War, focusing on Europe, where the Cold War once began and where it ended.

The present volume continues the analysis by widening the scope of the research project beyond Europe. It also discusses the nature of the emerging multipolar world system and its most immediate security-political repercussions. Change in the international system is finally becoming understood. The conceptual simplicity of the bipolar order has vanished, replaced by complexity. We are heading towards a multipolar system as well as towards a less stable peace.

I have drafted this book both in Bonn, Germany, and Helsinki, Finland. These two cities are the capitals of two countries which have greatly benefitted from the end of the Cold War. A totally new security environment is emerging in Europe, which is now more a part of a global and interdependent world system than before. The stability based on nuclear deterrence has gone, and no new global security system has yet emerged. I try to draw preliminary conclusions by discussing the ongoing change in geopolitical and geoeconomic terms. My primary assumption, which I believe is borne out on the following pages, is that the international system is heading toward new rivalry among a number of politico-economic power centers.

I am grateful to the editor of my books, Mr. Richard Levitt, whose analytical skills and vision have greatly contributed to the success of this project. Riku Warjovaara of the Finnish Institute of International Affairs provided invaluable help, and special thanks go to international relations specialist Jukka Salovaara, who has assisted me throughout the drafting process. Without many discussions with Jukka, I would not have reached the goal.

Alpo M. Rusi

1

Introduction

"The communities of mankind, like every human achievement and contrivance, are subject to endless variety and progression."
--Reinhold Niebuhr

"The international system of the 21st century will contain at least six major powers: the United States, Europe, China, Japan and probably India, as well as a multiplicity of medium-sized and smaller countries."
--Henry A. Kissinger

"Of the eight billion people expected to populate the earth by 2020, five billion will live in Asia, and of this, one billion will reside in 50 cities with more than 20 million inhabitants each."
--Riccardo Petrella[1]

This book is about the transition of the international system from bipolarity into a more complex, essentially multipolar, order. In this system, the key actors are powerful nations leading free-trade spaces, the latter of which will assume their roles as increasingly competitive politico-military blocs.[2] This historical development had its most visible manifestation when the Berlin Wall fell in 1989. That event presented symbolically a social revolution as well as one in international relations. While many of the trends and processes evident in Europe and in other continents before 1989 are present and will remain powerful for years to come, we are now better able to understand--in Joseph Nye's terms--that "the tectonic plates have shifted" in world politics as a result of the events of 1989-91.[3]

After the end of the Cold War, it was often repeated that the events of the end of the 1980s symbolized "something fundamental that happened in world history." Some observers concluded that the old political world map had become obsolete. Many agreed with Alvin and Heidi Toffler that "we are undergoing the deepest rearrangement of global power since the birth of industrial civilization."[4] There is certainly some truth in their proposition. The post-Cold War international system will be in a state of flux for many years to come. Order, admittedly tenuous during the Cold War, has given way to chaos in several parts of the globe. Consequently, with respect to the security policy repercussions of the end of the Cold War, idealists and realists have clashed in journals and governments alike.[5]

The immediate effects of these developments are obvious: German unification, liberation in Eastern Europe, and the spread of nationalistic and ethnic conflicts virtually throughout the globe but particularly in Europe. In the long term, however, the tectonic shift of plates, and its geopolitical repercussions, will be the most decisive feature of the systemic change. This turning point could be characterized as a departure from the American century and a heading towards the Asian and Pacific century. The sudden disappearance of the Soviet Union and the dramatic rise of China as an economic world power are the central factors of this change.[6]

Consequently, an assymetrical world system is now emerging as a configuration to replace the symmetrical Cold War bipolar structure. At this point, the United States remains the only true world power; it constitutes the core of a semi-unipolar but fragile order that is characterized by assymetries of global power divisions and economic resources. Yet its weaknesses are such that the post-Cold War "order" will not survive into the 21st century.[7] This book attempts to shed light on the overall development of the international system change and to make a forecast with respect to the security aspects of the rivalry between the emerging politico-economic blocs at the end of the 1990s and early 21st century.

As a result of the disappearance of the global ideological and political division, a new era of growing interdependence and globalization has really begun. The burgeoning economic and technological dynamism is a major unifying factor in the Pacific, Europe, and America alike, reshaping the interests, outlooks, and conceptions of security for a new generation of decision makers. Consequently, as Robert A. Manning states,

> the new logic of geoeconomics, and the imperatives flowing from the paramount importance attached to commercial and technological capacities, is pitted against the traditional logic of geopolitics: new requirements for partnership versus lingering suspicions and old ideas of nationhood.[8]

This geoeconomic logic also argues for a much-needed expansion of the definition of what constitutes security, and what has been termed "comprehensive security."

The liberalization of world trade and the increase of interdependence will also, however, accelerate the emergence of trade blocs in the longer term. This development results from the deepening and enlargement of regional integration. As one prominent observer, American scholar Jack Snyder, puts it: "This (regional integration) will continue from the Pacific Rim to the Baltic Rim. These regional arrangements and a strong multilateral system must be seen as complementary to each other." Snyder, however, adds that for the time being "the statistics do not support the contention that the world is headed toward a system of exclusive regional trading blocs."[9] This book makes the argument that although economic statistics do not yet necessarily support the argument of the emergence of trading blocs, geopolitical logic and power politics cannot be overlooked in the emerging international system. This ensuing political logic will strengthen the emergence of a multipolar order based on rival trade blocs centered on the big powers.

Behind the emerging trade blocs one can discover the principal nation-states of earlier centuries: Germany (the European Union), Russia (the Commonwealth of Independent States, the rump of the former Soviet Union), the United States (the North American Free Trade Agreement), and Japan as well as China (an East Asian economic area). Even a dynamic and economically powerful Japan is bound, however, to remain a "civilian power" overshadowed by China. The old Westphalian international system of nation-states has come only partly to its end. That system was well described by the great Austrian statesman Metternich, who argued that "the society of states is the essential condition of the modern world."[10] The international hierarchy and order of the Westphalian system were defined and redefined by hegemonic wars. Now it seems that this pattern has vanished. The hierarchy of the new "world order" is emerging primarily as a result of global political and economic processes, not military power and hegemonic wars. This "order" will still be based on the system of states, although forces and arrangements that are international or subnational will have increasing importance. As Max Singer and Aaron Wildavsky state, "within [the] broad structure, new patterns, not based on military power, will be increasingly important."[11] Great power rivalry will not vanish, although the conditions of the system may change and the actors may assume new roles and names.

This multidimensional rivalry is one of the basic preconditions for a dangerous peace over the longer term.[12]

This book does not share either the realist or idealist approach as such in discussing the conditions of peace within the forthcoming multipolar trade bloc order. In theoretical terms, the book deals with the interaction between economics and strategy in the emerging multipolar order. Beginning with the thesis that Paul Kennedy describes in his *Rise and Fall of the Great Powers* as the basic feature of the "modern," that is, post-Renaissance, period of international relations--"each of the leading states...strives to enhance its wealth and its power, to become (or to remain) both rich and strong"[13]--this research volume analyzes primarily the peace and security repercussions of the emerging new rivalry between the trade blocs of big powers within the ever present "modern" and conflictual period of the history of mankind. History has not ended, although it may take a new form.[14]

Moving on from Kennedy, the thesis of this book is that, barring deliberate management of international relations, the world will evolve into four or five politico-economic or cultural spaces or blocs, which will gradually become the chief dramatis personae on the global stage:

1. a European bloc (the European Union and its neighbors);
2. an East Asian bloc (around "a Greater China" and an East Asian economic area);
3. a Pan-American bloc (centered on the United States, with or without a North America Free Trade Agreement);
4. a Slavic and Orthodox Russian bloc (around the Moscow-led post-communist Russia); and
5. a Japanese-centered economic bloc (this one, however, may find itself in some kind of orbital relationship with the Chinese-led bloc).

The international system of the post-divisional economic interdependence--in other words, the globalization of market economy--as such may be developing toward a more stable and peaceful foundation. "There is virtually no conflict that a country can win that will do as much good for it as increasing its GNP by a percent or two for a few years," as two prominent scholars argue.[15] This imperative of "welfare over warfare" may be durable. Although the liberal democracies are presumably inclined to handle new economic conflicts peacefully, there is no certainty that a semi-democratic big power, let alone an authoritarian one, would limit promotion of its interests to peaceful means.[16] As a result, the emerging trading blocs will have to pursue security arrangements that to a great extent safeguard the traditional role of the nation-state. This book will therefore examine the international system change simultaneously through two distinct but intertwined theoretical concepts: geoeconomics and geopolitics.[17] However, the book makes an assumption that geoeconomics will be a more decisive factor relatively sooner, as these new-old power centers emerge during the era of increasing interdependence: "The economic foundations of political power are, in the long run, critically important determinants of changes in the great powers' pecking order," as Charles W. Kegley and Gregory A. Raymond conclude.[18] Geopolitics will, however, subsequently regain its primacy as a defining factor of international relations, and in particular relations between the new big powers, once the bloc consolidation is substantially complete.

Consequently, changes in power relations--and geopolitics--result mainly from the major changes of the power capacities, i.e., the economic foundations, of states. If there are too many "winners" and "losers" simultaneously in the international system, a conflictual situation, and even a war, may ensue.[19] Fundamental geopolitical transitions generally have only happened after hegemonic wars. Since the Cold War, however, the global geostrategic landscape has changed to a great extent peacefully. This process of geopolitical transition still continues, not simply at the European level, but, more dramatically, at the global level as well.[20]

The collapse of the Soviet imperium has created a power vacuum. This vacuum will be partly filled by the European Union in Eastern Euope, while in Asia it will be partly filled by China; furthermore, Islam, surging in various parts of the world and embracing a new international role, is also threatening Moscow's hold on its former and current satrapies.[21] Meanwhile, the disintegration of Russia itself will continue to the denigration of its global power status. However, it would be wrong to insist that Russia is doomed to lose all of its world reach.

In the longer term, however, the real hierarchy of the system will be defined primarily by the combination of the military might, geographic location and economic capacities of the big powers. Therefore, the United States, China, Japan, the European states (European Union), Russia, perhaps one of the big developing countries (such as India) or some Islamic grouping should gradually gain the leading positions within the emerging multipolar order.[22]

In the 20th century, security has traditionally been the product of the balance of power. The international community has had to "balance" Germany twice, then had to contain the Soviet Union by the same means during the Cold War era. Now this community is facing a more difficult task: It has to create stability in a cooperative--not confrontational--mode in global terms; moreover, such balances as are struck will now have to struck more *among* regions, not simply *within* them.[23]

As a research method, the book uses the periodizing of developments: the period of transition, the emergence of the multipolar order, and finally, the forecast of the security repercussions of the expected rivalry between four or five big powers. It discusses the foundations and prospects of regionalism, and its "soft" (viz., economic) and "hard" (politico-military) forms. The book attempts to formulate a global approach to the international system change described as a transition from the post-Cold War "disorder" to an emerging multipolar order. Although one of book's key theses derives from rivalry between big powers, it does not necessarily predict the repetition previous patterns of confrontation, such as the Long Cycle and hegemonic war.[24] The security development of the emerging multipolar order will have more alternatives, although the plethora of options available to the actors could make for a dangerous peace. Readers will find, for example, that I am in agreement with Miles Kahler, who believes that the successful completion of the Uruguay Round negotiations and the creation of the World Trade Organization suggest that regionalism and global governance need not conflict.[25]

The book focuses mainly on Europe, Russia, North America and Asia. I will only briefly discuss Africa or Latin America. While this is not meant to underestimate their importance, these two continents play only side-roles in the overall development of my arguments.

Africa certainly has new hope with the democratization of South Africa, which will contribute to the growth and development of the whole region. Africa is, however, likely to be a passive actor in the international order, riddled as it is with internal political and economic problems. Latin America has stabilized and is likely to develop further with more stable political regimes. It is, however, distant from the centers of world politics and likely to be a junior partner in a grouping with North America.

It could even happen that Latin America and Africa will profit from the emerging system of New Rivalry, where North America, Europe, Russia, Japan and China are central actors. Outside or distant to the new international rivalry, Africa and Latin America may develop peacefully and successfully while others compete between each other.

Notes

1. Reinhold Niebuhr, *Nations and Empires: Recurring Patterns in the Political Order* (London: Faber and Faber), 1960. p. 1; Henry A. Kissinger, *Diplomacy* (New York: Simon & Schuster), 1994, pp. 23-24; Riccardo Petrella, "A Global Agora vs. Gated City-Republics," *New Perspectives Quarterly*, Winter 1995, pp. 21-22.

2. See, for example, Deepak Lal, "Trade Blocs and Multipolar Free Trade," *Journal of Common Market Studies*, Number 3, 1993, pp. 349-358. Lal makes the argument that there is the current prospect "of a strengthening of regional trading blocs at the expense of the multilateral trading system."

3. Joseph Nye, "American Strategy After Bipolarity," *International Affairs*, Number 3, 1990, p. 513.

4. Alvin Toffler and Heidi Toffler, "Mapping out a Trisected World," *International Herald Tribune*, November 5, 1993.

5. For the opening statement of this debate, see Francis Fukuyama, "The End of History," *The National Interest*, Summer 1989. Fukuyama argued that democratic values and market economy have become universal, which meant that the era of ideological struggle dating back to the French Revolution had ended. This kind of idealistic euphoria was attacked most conspicuously by John J. Mearsheimer in *"Back to the Future: Instability in Europe After the Cold War,"* *International Security*, Summer 1990.

6. The argument of the transition of trading blocs into political powers was put by *The Economist* (January 8, 1994) in a very simplistic but visionary manner: "A strong America, an advancing China, a struggling Russia and an uncertain Europe make up the new quartet of big powers. The interplay of their interests and the threat of proliferation will fix the rudiments of the next world order."

7. See Christopher Layne, "The Unipolar Illusion," *International Security*, Vol. 17, 1993. My book stresses that the idea of the international system remains always to a certain extent abstract, descriptive and theoretical. The system has among its subsystems a set of actors (states, like Russia, China and the United States, or communities of states, like the European Union). A major work about the international system is by Morton Kaplan, *System and Process in International Politics* (New York: John Wiley & Sons), 1957. Kaplan's analysis has been subject to strong criticism by a number of scholars. The term "world order," as the author of this book uses it, signifies an analytical structure that makes possible understanding and prediction, hence policy and diplomacy. The current transitory order (or the new "disorder") is based primarily on the system

of states.

8. Robert A. Manning, "The Asian Paradox: Toward a New Architecture," *World Policy Journal*, Summer 1993.

9. Jack Snyder, "The New Nationalism: Realist Interpretations and Beyond," in Richard Rosecrance and Anthony A. Stein (eds.), *The Domestic Bases of Grand Strategy* (Ithaca, NY: Cornell University Press), 1993, pp. 179-200. Quoted from an address by the Finnish OECD ambassador Pasi Rutanen, *"The Tripolar World: The Dangers of Fragmentation and the Role of the OECD,"* World Affairs Council of San Antonio (Texas), January 13, 1994.

10. Quoted from Fareed Zakaria, "Is Realism Finished?" *The National Interest*, Winter 1992/93, pp. 21-31. As to the concept of the Westphalian international system and the foundations of peace during that period of 350 years, see Kalevi J. Holsti, *Peace and War: Armed Conflicts and International Order 1648-1989* (Cambridge: Cambridge University Press), 1991.

11. Max Singer and Aaron Wildavsky, *The Real World Order: Zones of Peace, Zones of Turmoil* (London: Chatham House Publishers), 1993.

12. See Gerald Segal, "The Coming Confrontation Between China and Japan," *World Policy Journal*, Summer 1993. For an interesting prediction of the future shape of the international system of five power centers (China, Russia, the European Union, Japan and the United States), see Helmut Schmidt, "Die nahe Zukunft: der Ferne Osten," *Die Zeit*, November 26, 1993.

13. Paul Kennedy, *The Rise and Fall of the Great Powers* (London: Random House Publishers), 1987.

14. Regarding the emergence of a world economy, see Immanuel Wallerstein, *The Modern World System: Capitalist Agriculture and the Origins of the European World Economy in the Sixteenth Century* (New York: Academic Press), 1974. See also Aristide R. Zollberg, "Origins of the Modern World System: A Missing Link," *World Politics*, 1981, who states that Wallerstein makes a systematic error throughout his book by neglecting the political structures and processes. The present book tries to combine both political and economic processes and structures.

15. Singer and Wildavsky, *The Real World Order*, p. 26.

16. On the emergence of a conflictual world disorder after the end of the Cold War, see my article "Regional Stability in the Post-Cold War Era," in *Yearbook of Finnish Foreign Policy* (Helsinki: Finnish Institute of International Affairs), 1991. As to the prospects for a peaceful post-Cold War order, see Bruce Russett, *Grasping the Democratic Peace: Principles for a Post-Cold War World*, (Princeton: Princeton University Press), 1993.

17. Edward Luttwak coined the phrase "geoeconomics" in "From Geopolitics to Geo-economics," *The National Interest*, Summer 1990. For a brief but comprehensive analysis about the concepts of geoeconomics and geopolitics, see Michael P. Gerace, "Transforming the Pattern of Conflict: Geopolitics and Post-Cold War Europe," *Comparative Strategy*, Volume 11, 1992.

18. Charles W. Kegley, Jr. and Gregory A. Raymond, *A Multipolar Peace? Great-Power Politics in the Twenty-first Century* (New York: St. Martin's Press), 1994.

19. As to "winners" and "losers" of the international system change, see, e.g., Paul Kennedy, *Preparing for the Twenty-first Century* (New York: Random House), 1993, or Alfred Zänker, *Epoche der Entscheidungen: Deutschland, Eurasien und die Welt von Morgen* (Asendorf: MUT-Verlag), 1992.

20. As to the concept of geopolitical transition, see Peter J. Taylor, *Britain and the Cold War: 1945 as a Geopolitical Transition* (London: Pinter Publishers), 1990.

21. I have dealt with the immediate geostrategic implications of the end of the Cold War in my book *After the Cold War: Europe's New Political Architecture* (London: Macmillan; New York: St. Martin's Press), 1991. As to the emerging new geostrategic role of Russia as a "buffer" vis-a-vis the revolutionary Muslim states, see Vladimir Baranovsky and Hans-Joachim Spanger (eds.), *In From the Cold: Germany, Russia and the Future of Europe* (Boulder, CO: Westview Press), 1993. Concerning the Islamic challenge itself, see, for example, Singer and Wildavsky, *The Real World Order,* 1993.

22. In 1993 in connection with the Asia-Pacific summit the Clinton administration argued for the deepening of US relations with the Pacific and Asian states by emphasizing "natural," not strategic, causes. The Asia-Pacific region had become the most dynamic component of the world economy in the late 1980s and early 1990s. As a background analysis, see "Now Let's Build an Asian-Pacific Economic Community," an excerpt from a confidential report to the Asia-Pacific summit meeting in Seattle in November 1994 published in *International Herald Tribune,* November 4, 1994. China, however, will be a *strategic* challenge to the United States in the 1990s. See Michael T. Klare, "The Next Great Arms Race," *Foreign Affairs,* Volume 72, 1993.

23. As to the need to develop the concept of security "beyond the balance of power," see Daniel N. Nelson, "Great Powers and World Peace," in Michael T. Klare and Daniel C. Thomas (eds.), *World Security: Challenges for a New Century* (New York: St. Martin's Press), 1993.

24. For a discussion of Long Cycle theory, see George Modelski, *Long Cycles in World History* (London: Macmillan), 1987.

25. For a comprehensive study of the emerging post-Cold War multipolar world order, see Kegley and Raymond, *A Multipolar Peace?* which considers how regional alliances, the UN, and other international organizations might have a role in minimizing conflict in the multipolar world. Additionally, see Miles Kahler, "A World of Blocs," *World Policy Journal,* Spring 1995, pp. 19-27.

2

Collapsing Bipolarity

"The fall of the Berlin Wall in November 1989 can be taken as the symbolic end of an era in world affairs in which major events fell under the ominous shadow of the Cold War, with its constant threat of nuclear annihilation. That conventional picture is certainly not false, but it is nevertheless partial and misleading. By uncritically adopting it, we seriously misunderstand the recent past, and are not well-situated to comprehend what lies ahead."

--Noam Chomsky

"The new world order has to find institutions and mechanisms similar to what the creators of the post-World War II international order founded in the period from 1945 to 1950. The possibilities for creativity are greater than they were then, though the beginnings of the solutions are not yet as obvious."

--Henry A. Kissinger[1]

The End of the Cold War

"This is just the end of the beginning."

--Winston Churchill

The end of the Cold War has been usually related to the end of the division of Germany in 1989-90. Furthermore, it is widely agreed that this period of the post-Cold War "New World Order" was over by the middle of the 1990s. At this juncture, it became obvious to the "winners" of the Cold War how difficult it was to manage this new order. In his 1992 book *The United States and the End of the Cold War,* the eminent diplomatic historian John Lewis Gaddis posited that the trouble with victory is that it tends to produce power imbalances. The peace settlements of 1815 and 1945 were expressly designed to reincorporate the defeated powers back into the international system as quickly as possible after a

11

rehabilitative period. It is no coincidence that they were the two most durable peace settlements of modern times.

It first looked as if the transition from the Yalta order--bipolarity--to the Malta order--multipolarity--constituted a major step toward a just and lasting peace. In the history of Europe, no such profound geopolitical transition had ever taken place without a hegemonic war. The war in ex-Yugoslavia and in a number of former Soviet states justified fears, however, that the road toward a lasting peace would be more rocky than expected. The world after the Cold War became *sui generis*, and power is becoming more multidimensional, structures more complex and states themselves more permeable.

One can try to elaborate on the failures of the international community to manage the end of the Cold War. As Gaddis argues, perhaps this is "because the communist regimes of the Soviet Union and Eastern Europe have not actually suffered a military defeat, we in the West are not focusing as carefully as we should on the problems of reconstruction and reintegration in that part of the world."[2] We do not know the answer, but after the post-Cold War period of about five years, no new and stable peace order has emerged to replace the rather stable bipolarity.

Geopolitics Revisited

Geopolitics has perhaps been underestimated as an analytical tool, condemned as unsuitable for the modern era of globalization and transnational corporations. The "geopolitics" school of realist thought and political geography generally direct attention to the influence of geographic factors on national power and international conduct. Therefore, geopolitics is only one aspect of the external environment that may influence states' foreign policies. A reappraisal of geopolitics is long overdue, however, and in the next chapter I make my own sketch of modern geopolitics, which attempts to give due respect to the structural transformation of the world through globalization.

This chapter deals with the geopolitical transition of 1989-91. The collapse of bipolarity is analyzed in terms of changes in power relations. The debate on the consequences of the end of the Cold War demonstrates how two opposed schools of thought--or analytical tribes--clash without, however, providing a synthesis as a guide. One camp sees no basic change in European politics since the creation of the nation-state. The other claims that Europe has escaped from its perpetual wars because of economic globalization, integration and common values. The truth lies somewhere in between and its search should not be abandoned for the sake of theoretical parsimony.

Geopolitics is the spatial study of the relationships among states and the implications of these relationships for the morphology of the political map as a whole. In the 1990s, the two most clearly perceptible levels of geopolitical reality are--still--the nation-state and--increasingly--the global totality, and explanatory models and theories have been produced for both. In this book, the global totality is referred to as the "world system" or "international system." The world system can be seen in terms of geography of economic development combined simultaneously with geography of politico-military development.[3] Modern geopolitical analysis attempts to transcend a day-to-day commentary of current affairs and seeks to find a structure underlying world politics. While the global economy is notoriously cyclical, patterns of political power and national interest, being sometimes surprisingly stable, seem to resist being reduced to cycles.

I assume that any analysis of geopolitical systems cannot afford to avoid Sir Halford Mackinder and his "Heartland Theory." According to Mackinder, the mastery of the Eurasian heartland, or "world island," is the key to world power. The geopolitical struggle is bound to be a competition, with land and maritime powers contending for the prize, Eurasia.[4]

Different actors have assumed the roles of these players in history. Early in this century, Wilhelmine Germany sought mastery of the heartland, opposed most vigorously by Britain, the chief maritime power. More recently, during the Cold War, the Soviet Union was the land power challenged by the maritime power of the United States. In the coming decades, we may perhaps witness a struggle over this heartland between Russia and China, with Western powers--America, Western Europe and Japan--playing the part of the maritime power.

Two geopolitical orders have prevailed in the 20th century: the Order of British Succession, which lasted from 1907 to 1946, and the Cold War Order, which began approximately in 1947 and ended most definitively in 1989. The implicit aim of the first was to control German expansionism while Britain's power declined. Two "German wars" were fought because of this--the First and the Second World Wars. The dominant logic, or organizing principle, of the Cold War Order was a balance of power between the two superpowers.

The phases between such orders, geopolitical transitions, are periods in which competing nascent or declining orders co-exist. The outcome of these transitions is seldom predetermined or straight. Smooth transitions from one order to another are rare. In the words of Peter J. Taylor: "Geopolitical transitions are pre-eminently fluid periods of international relations when different geopolitical options are vying for construction."[5]

During transitions, visions of a coming order are highly speculative, resting on historical precedents and analysis of structural change. Historical precedents cannot be taken at face value, and their relevance in today's world must be constantly re-evaluated. However, precursors of the new order usually exist within the old one. In our search for a geopolitical order for the post-Cold War world, we must closely examine the current order to discern within it elements of continuity and of change.

Many critics of geopolitical analysis of world politics believe such examination lacks appreciation for economic reality. This need not be the case. Geopolitics has to be complemented by geoeconomics, an analysis of how economic factors influence state behavior, state interests and, consequently, geopolitics. A structural transformation of the international economy is apparent. Economic actors are less dependent on the state than previously and there is a strong case for speaking about a global economy and transnational production. States and markets are thus part of a larger "dialectical" struggle which can be viewed through the prism of a broadly defined geopolitical context.

In his analysis of the geopolitical transition from the Order of British Succession to the Cold War Order, Taylor stresses that there were at least five possible outcomes: a world where the Grand Alliance of the United States, Soviet Union and Britain would remain intact; an amicable division of the world into American, British and Soviet spheres of influence, or pan-regions; an anti-imperial alliance between the United States and the Soviet Union in opposition to European colonialist powers; an anti-hegemonic front between the Soviet Union and a Laborite Britain to oppose the United States; and an anti-communist front dividing the world into two.[6]

The anti-communist front was the order that emerged. This outcome was, however, only one of several different options and it came into being through, amongst other things, hard work by the British to "remain at the table" as a junior partner to the United States rather than be excluded from influence altogether by an amicable power-sharing arrangement between the two superpowers. This outcome was not self-evident in the years of transition 1945-1947. Britain's renunciation of responsibility for settling Greece's civil war in 1947 could have been interpreted as an admission of inability to influence events in Europe, a result of exhaustion following its heroic anti-Axis efforts. Thus its successful campaign to remain a "world power" (at least until the Suez Crisis ten years later) is an example of fruitful political and diplomatic effort. It serves as an example. During our current transitory phase, we must remember that political choices influence events and the shaping of the coming order is not beyond our means. The necessary corollary is that we must be aware of existing alternatives and competing paths to the 21st century.

Geopolitical codes--or modes of action--are apparent in the actions of states. Three levels of code exist: local, regional, and global.[7] By analyzing these codes, we may gain an appreciation of how global powers may react during geopolitical transition and what are the crucial factors in determining the new geopolitical order.

Post-Cold War Geopolitics in Transition

"Just as the fall of the Berlin Wall in November 1989 marked the end of the old contest between capitalism and communism, so the integration of the European Common Market, on January 1, 1993, will mark the beginning of a new economic contest in a new century at the start of the third millennium. At that moment, for the first time in more than a century, the United States will become the second largest economy in the world. This reality will become the symbol for the start of the competition that determines who will own the twenty-first century."

--Lester Thurow[8]

All geopolitical orders contain novel or alien elements which reflect a change in the disposition of forces and thus signal the direction for new geopolitical orders to come. Winston Churchill is apocryphally credited with the adage that the essence of genius lies in turning the inevitable to advantage. Churchill, however, spent years trying to stave off the inevitable--viz., Britain's imperial decline. A better example of diplomatic tea-leaf reading, and consequent exploitation of changing circumstance, was the foreign policy of US President Richard Nixon and his chief advisor, Dr. Henry Kissinger.

The foreign policy of President Nixon stemmed from his recognition that, while the world geopolitical system was bipolar and the United States had to focus its energies on containment of Soviet influence, economic reality was increasingly multipolar. The United States was no longer the economic and financial giant it had once been. On the contrary, the Vietnam War had helped propel the American economy into unforeseen troubles, finally leading to the demise of its financial hegemony; this in turn prompted the collapse of the US-led "Bretton Woods" international economic system in the early 1970s. The subsequent oil shock signified an unprecedented challenge to US industrial competitiveness--a challenge it assumed poorly.

The Nixon/Kissinger foreign policy vision was the recognition that the United States would have to come to terms with a multipolar geopolitical system sooner or later. From their perspective, the sooner it did so, the easier the transition would be. Britain had only conceded its leading role after virtually draining its national resources during two world wars. Nixon and Kissinger were determined that the United States would avoid the same mistake.

In this conception, the United States and the Soviet Union would have to live with China, Western Europe, and Japan as equal, or at least near-equal, powers. Kissinger had the diplomacy of European great powers of the 1800s in mind when he sketched the world to be and the consequent policies of the United States, which more clearly than ever before would be premised on American geopolitical interest rather than the messianism or exceptionalism that had nominally been the previous determinant.

The conciliation with China was a spectular achievement, giving the United States considerable strategic advantage at virtually no cost. The basic idea was that Washington should be closer to both Moscow and Beijing than these two poles of the communist world were to each other. Kissinger and Nixon thus placed the United States as the fulcrum in the delicate diplomatic balance between the Soviet Union and China. (This is a position it continues to occupy over 20 years later. Hearkening back to Mackinder, then, in the coming geopolitical order, the United States will remain the balancer between China and Russia, geopolitical rivals for the heartland. The geopolitical interest of the United States is to keep Moscow and Beijing apart, regardless of the political direction Russia follows and the trends that emerge in post-Deng China.)

While the characterization of previous US foreign policy as heavily grounded in ideology may be inaccurate (and thus the emphasis or interest in Nixon's policies less innovative than it would appear), the overt concept of balancing was relatively novel. The Nixonian view of world politics drew from the Concert of Europe of the 19th century, where roughly equal powers balanced each other through shifting alliances. To defend its interests in a pluralistic world, the United States would have to safeguard its basic geopolitical interests by a changing pattern of alliances, clever diplomacy and well planned use of force commensurate with its resources.[9] But transitions in geopolitical code are no smoother than they are for geopolitical circumstance. After several years of detente provided breathing space for instituting such a concept of balance, the United States and the Soviets headed towards a new confrontation, the so-called Second Cold War, in the 1980s. For nearly 20 more years, bipolar rivalry continued, its endgame obscuring to most observers the change in "the correlation of forces" (a term beloved by Soviet diplomatic theorists) that pointed the way toward multipolarity. It can be asked whether this confrontation actually was in US interests: Would a smoother transition of the bipolar order rather than its collapse been better for world stability? Did the United States support Mikhail Gorbachev, who presided over the demise of the Soviet Union, for the sake of stability or because of a lack of analysis?

The Soviet reaction to the structural geopolitical shift of forces was evident from the end of the 1960s. During the decade, the Soviet Union was at the height of its economic force. There was even talk of surpassing capitalism in its economic achievements and the Soviet standard of living was decent, if far from affluent. By the 1970s, however, the growth rate of the Soviet economy showed signs of stalling. The system was becoming obsolete to a great extent because of global technological and economic change. Based on rigid central control, it could not cope with the information revolution, which was transforming Western economies and societies, leaving the Soviet bloc far behind. The Soviet Union had to do something to safeguard its strategic achievements.

It was clear that the comparative slide of the Soviet economy would sooner or later damage its strategic position. Moscow's plan to avoid this was to find a political arrangement with the West that would guarantee the strategic achievements of the Second World War and help renovate the Soviet economy. The specific goal was the project on a European Peace Treaty, which finally led to the CSCE process in the 1970s.

The Second World War had ended without a formal peace treaty, as the victorious grand alliance fell into disagreement soon after German and Japanese surrender. The division of Europe hardened, and the United States and Soviet Union were left with their own blocs to manage.

However, as the Soviet Union was gradually losing its comparative power position--which must have been even more apparent to the Soviet leadership than to the West, which failed to appreciate the true condition of the Soviet economy--it became crucial to consolidate supremacy in Eastern Europe with Western recognition by means of a peace treaty.

Western powers were reluctant to recognize definitively the Soviet sphere of influence and supremacy over Eastern Europe. The process later known as the Conference on Security and Cooperation in Europe (CSCE) became the substitute for a peace treaty. CSCE initially satisfied the Soviets by recognizing the immutability of borders, a concept dear to Soviet leaders aware of their weakness, and by laying a framework for economic cooperation, deemed necessary for the renovation of the Soviet economy. The West did not accede to Soviet demands for free. For the West, the biggest achievement of CSCE was its human rights dimension. The Soviet Union and its satellites were forced to recognize human rights, including free speech and free movement, for their citizens, although the recognition was extremely qualified and limited in effect. Nevertheless, in signing the CSCE Final Document in Helsinki in 1975, Moscow explicitly conceded--although it continually contested--the right of all CSCE participating states to interest themselves in the maintenance and protection of those rights in every CSCE country. This became a crucial mechanism in the latter transformation of socialist states. It can be said that the seeds of the European upheavals of 1989-91 were sown by the CSCE.[10]

From the Soviet point of view, the CSCE was a mechanism to safeguard the European status quo and consequently keep Soviet power in Europe at an all-time high. Furthermore, the Soviet Union tried to have better access to western technology through the CSCE. How ironic that the CSCE became increasingly a mechanism for political change in socialist countries from within, which undermined the division of Europe and Russian supremacy over half of the continent. The Russian failure to manage a smooth transition out of the bipolar order was even more glaring than the American.

The Collapse of the Bipolar System

The Cold War was a bipolar system, where two opposed superpowers formed a stable balance of power, which was in turn strengthened by existential nuclear deterrence. The end of the bipolar division was an exceptional event in history in that it happened peacefully, without a hegemonic war. Basically, the bipolar system ended as its Soviet pillar collapsed from within.

Detente in the 1970s can be interpreted as a partial recognition by both superpowers, that they could not--for entirely different sets of reasons--stay on top forever. A moderation of the superpower rivalry was in their mutual interest, as it was becoming apparent that there was no end in sight other than mutual annihilation. Military rivalry was also becoming an economic burden for both. However, the tentative rapprochement--which might have been used by the two to redefine thoroughly their relationship--came to an end due to Soviet attempts to take advantage of detente by extending influence in the third world and seeking strategic gains in Europe. It is possible that, with a weak Brezhnev at its head, the Soviet political leadership could not match the power of the Soviet military-industrial complex, which needed rivalry and conquest for its existence and power.

In the late 1970s and early 1980s, the Soviet Union adopted new intermediate-range missile systems (the SS-20s, which threatened the balance of power in Europe), intervened in Afghanistan, forced the imposition of martial law in Poland, embarked on new adventures in the third world, and threatened US naval supremacy by developing a global blue water navy. The United States reacted to the Soviet strategic challenge by massive rearmament, which finally contributed to the collapse of the Soviet economy. In the early 1980s, the administration of President Ronald Reagan launched an unprecedented military build-up: New intermediate-range missiles were installed in Europe, the US Navy was to be developed into a 600-fighting ship force, and strategic nuclear forces were upgraded. One of the most prominent programs was the "Star Wars" strategic defense initiative (SDI), which aimed at a high technology-based interception system against Soviet nuclear missiles. Countering this massive program would only exacerbate the strains under which the Soviet economy was already laboring.

Perestroika and glasnost, advocated by Mikhail Gorbachev, were, inter alia, attempts to reform the Soviet economy. As an essential prerequisite for economic reforms, conciliation with the United States was sought in order to stop the arms race. One important aspect of perestroika was economic reform in Eastern Europe. The lion's share of Soviet trade was with its COMECON partners, who among other things supplied the Soviet Union with vital industrial components and consumer goods.

In the Soviet perception, economic reform in the countries of Eastern Europe would have enhanced the Soviets' own reforms by increasing provision of both kinds of products, thus making Soviet consumers happy and helping the Soviet economy develop. However, economic reform in Eastern Europe lead to unintended results contrary to Soviet basic interests, as had the CSCE. Reform also had political consequences, which in both the USSR and its satellites opened the doors for pluralistic political culture and the collapse of the authority of party rule. Making virtue of necessity, the Soviet leadership could do nothing but jettison the Brezhnev Doctrine, by which they had arrogated to themselves the right to protect the advance of socialism in "fraternal" countries and to dictate the course of political developments there. Its replacement: the Sinatra Doctrine (so called by Soviet spokesman Gennadi Gerasimov, paraphrasing the song lyrics made famous by the American singer--"I Did It My Way"), which recognized the right of Eastern European satellites to reform. Gorbachev did not intentionally dismantle the Soviet system, but his reform policies resulted in just that.

With the collapse of communism in sight, the German question came to the fore. From a geopolitical point of view, the division of Germany became obsolete, as one power pole in this division lost its grip on Central Europe. But if no division, whither Germany? And whither Europe? For decades, leaders on both sides, fearing the answers, had been content to let the artificial divide remain a rhetorical sticking point between them; no one had actually tried to resolve the issues. Even the Germans themselves had appeared content at superficial, rather than structural, attempts at conciliation. Willy Brandt, West German chancellor in the late 1960s and early 1970s, was the lone exception among statesmen in either the East or the West who made serious efforts to attack the root causes for the division. He had been saluted by his foreign contemporaries, but he had not been joined--or completely trusted--by them.

The unification of Germany, in fact, revealed the geopolitical codes of the major European actors. The prospect of a unified and strong Germany--and renewal of its role as a European great power--initially prompted France and Britain into historically familiar patterns of action. Britain tried desperately to prevent German reunification in order to keep its historical rival divided and weak. During the fall of 1989 Prime Minister Margaret Thatcher was a strong advocate of maintaining the status quo by keeping East Germany intact. Meanwhile, France tried to make arrangements over Germany's head with its historical ally against the Germans, Russia (then still the Soviet Union). President François Mitterrand met the Soviet leader Gorbachev in Minsk in an attempt to fashion a Franco-Russian bilateral entente over the German question in December 1989. Later, when German unification became inevitable, France took steps to form a mini-coalition to balance Germany by upgrading links with Central European countries, particularly Czechoslovakia, in a policy reminiscent of French "Little Entente" strategy before the Second World War. The Gallic attempts were no more successful in the 1990s than they had been in the late 1930s. In some respects, France, like the Soviet Union, is one of the "losers" at the end of the Cold War. Like Russia, France will have to reconcile its global self-image with a new regional role.

The United States' position finally sealed the unification of Germany and presented Britain and France with a fait accompli. The American post-war geopolitical code regarding the German question had not been to keep Germany weak but rather to keep it on the side of the United States and thus prevent this economic giant from turning against its ally. Germany could have been weakened in a lasting way under, for example, the relatively punitive program suggested by US Treasury Secretary Henry Morgenthau after the Second World War, which would have prevented German re-industrialization and made Germany into a huge non-industrial agrarian zone. But a more prescient approach, conceived by senior State Department planner George Kennan, was adopted instead. Kennan identified four advanced industrial regions which could threaten the United States: Britain, Germany, Japan and the Soviet Union. The idea of containment was thus to keep Britain, Germany and Japan firmly in the US camp.[11]

Once the German unification process had begun, US support was unequivocal. France and Britain could do little to influence events. They had to make the best out of a situation basically agreed between the United States and Germany. The French in particular pursued a deepening of European integration--if Germany could not be kept divided, it should be economically and politically more integrated into common institutions. Within an "ever closer union" (to use the words associated with former French Premier Edouard Balladur) featuring a Common Foreign and Security Policy and a European Defense Identity (all envisioned the Treaty of Maastricht), Germany would be able to exercise its increased powers, but only together with other West European states. Complementarily, the envisioned Economic and Monetary Union would mean that the monetary might of the Bundesbank would be shared with Germany's European partners.

The expectations related to the New Europe were at first positive. The end of superpower rivalry opened the possibility for agreement on previously unreconciliable issues (inter alia, to change borders by peaceful means). Common institutions could be strengthened and a strong role for the CSCE (renamed in December 1994 the Organization of Security and Cooperation in Europe--OSCE) was planned. In the New Europe, even the notion of security changed. During the Cold War, security had been a matter of preventing states from attacking each other. This was achieved with mutual deterrence, as not even a "small" interstate conflict could begin in Europe without leading to, at the very least, superpower involvement and the implicit risk of escalation to the nuclear level.

In the new Europe, local conflicts were no longer aspects of the superpower balance of forces. Thus fighting could occur without risk of nuclear escalation. War soon broke out in former Yugoslavia and parts of the Confederation of Independent States (CIS). To date, these conflicts have remained, however, predominantly local and it would seem that for the immediate future threats to European security will derive primarily from sub-state problems emerging from local instability.

With no basic disagreements between European powers, common efforts were made to control the conflicts: the OSCE and the United Nations both attempted to resolve the ex-Yugoslav conflict, albeit with poor results. While, from the point of view of established states, war is a common problem that everybody wishes to avoid, like a vicious epidemy to be contained by common measures, it should be asked whether the continued failure to obtain satisfactory ends will lead to a diminution of these common interests in favor of more divergent ones.

Moreover, Western Europe is broadening integration. The European Union is in the process of enlargement--Austria, Finland, and Sweden became new members in January 1995--which should further strengthen the Union as a new center for all of Europe. Cynically, one could argue that the net containing Germany has been stretched wider as a result of unification. Alternatively, the increased economic potential and resources of the larger EU also make it that much more an appealing partner for East European states.

These latter states are developing links with the European Union. The most advanced ones have Europe Agreements with the Union, which improve market access and open political consultations. Russia and other members of the CIS have Partnership and Cooperation Agreements, which form a more distanced partnership with the European Union.

Because in extremis the Soviet Union was weak, it had to be content with the honorable exit it was offered (sweetened by the economic favors granted by Germany) from Eastern Europe. For the Soviets (and for the Russians), the region has been paramount for security. Twice in this century alone, Eastern Europe has been an invasion route into Russia. It remains to be seen if the unification of Germany means that Russia's geopolitical code has changed--from a western threat perception to a southern one, for instance--or that it was just a consequence of its decline and transformation from a global to a regional power.

Despite the above, Russia will play a decisive role in *European* power politics for years to come. Ukraine (or at least parts of it, such as Crimea) and Belarus may reintegrate with Russia politically and economically. It it clear that the development of Russia--and its role within the European system--will have influence on European developments at large. But economic reforms are slow, and results are even slower. Economic difficulties and uncertainty are hard on the Russian electorate. This has produced strong extremist political movements, which, if they were voted into power, could threaten the course of reform.

What motivates Russian foreign policy and strategic vision? In what direction are they heading? Since the end of the Cold War, Russian foreign policy has been generally moderate, but that may be the fruit of diplomatic ambivalence or schizophrenia rather than conscious orientation. Indeed, there has been no great show of commitment to a direction, any direction. In the early 1990s, Russia wanted closer and cooperative links with the West. By 1993, however, hints of a new Russian policy could be seen: Russia began to consolidate its influence in the CIS and had realized that its interests and views did not always coincide with Western ones.

Ex-Yugoslavia is a good example of the confused nature of the country's policies. Russia first sided with the Serbs and condemned Western action. In 1994, though, Russia slowly approached the Western position (itself hardly a paragon of consistency), but maintained a certain distance.

Russian domestic politics certainly seem to have an influence on foreign policy. The rise of nationalistic political movements has constrained President Boris Yeltsin, who seems to be forced to echo some of their views in order to keep his grip on political power. Hence his statement in late 1994 at the CSCE summit in Budapest that the international situation was turning towards a "Cold Peace"--with Russia being unfavorably treated. Yet even though Russia's war with Chechnya strengthened the nationalist mood of many Kremlin leaders in early 1995, this "Russian revivalism" is still rhetoric intended to appease ultra-nationalists rather than serve as a policy lodestar. Russian foreign policy is still cooperation-minded and certainly not anti-western. This may change if ultra-nationalists gain the presidency. Regardless of who holds the reins of power, Russia remains a question mark to be further analyzed. Is Russia a Slavic neo-imperialist entity or a fragmenting post-imperialist one?

Back to the Future or a New European Peace Order?

The debate on the implications of the end of the Cold War in Europe can be roughly bracketed by its extremes: *Back to the Future pessimism*, as laid out by John J. Mearsheimer, and *End of History optimism*, well presented in Francis Fukuyama's famous argument.[12]

The prevailing interpretation of Fukuyama perhaps gives less than due credit to his ideas, which were foresighted when he made his case. However, Fukuyama's work has become a high-water mark of the hopes that prevailed with the demise of the artificial and ideological division of the European continent. This optimism maintained that the collapse of communism signified a universal acceptance of liberalism as an ideological order in which no conflicts would arise, as the values and goals in different societies would be identical. A shared ideological system and ensuing common norms would guarantee a non-conflictual future. Competition would be a matter of economic enterprise within agreed bounds, and would always redound to the benefit of the individual.

Such optimism was even reflected for a while in US policy towards Eastern Europe. Attempts were made to tie economic assistance to the development of the private sector, which would strengthen liberal elements in society against the last vestiges of central authority. More broadly, George Bush's New World Order--which would have given the United States leadership in world affairs, because End of History is linked to ideas of universal (that is to say, American) values--can be interpreted as one variation on Fukuyama's theme.

Another variation was the emergence of a stable and peaceful system in Europe. Eastern Europe would adopt democratic political systems and embrace market economies. This was actually done in words at the Paris summit of all CSCE heads of state in October 1990 through the Charter for a New Europe, which officially signified the end of the Cold War. However, the translation of words into deeds remains unaccomplished. The transition to democracy and market economy has proved to be a rocky road with many potential detours.

Fukuyama's optimism and its variants rested on unrealistic assumptions. In reality, there is no consensus over values, the transition to democracy and market economy in Eastern Europe is far from smooth, and the end result there will in any event reflect local conditions rather than be a straightforward copy of western systems. According to American academic Jack Snyder, End of History was a case of ideological wishful thinking and political rhetoric rather than a serious analytical position on European change.[13]

At the other end of the analytic spectrum, Back to the Future pessimism argued that the stable bipolar system would be replaced by a more unstable system, leading either to war, or, in historical terms, to the pre-1914 era of European politics. Mearsheimer holds true to Kenneth Waltz's view of world politics, which, seeing the international structure as the chief determinant feature of the system, posits that the more units a system has, the more unstable it will be. Thus a bipolar structure, where a balance of power is easily achieved, is more unstable than any system with more components. John Lewis Gaddis is roughly on the same lines when he analyzes the Cold War as a Long Peace, wherein bipolarity guaranteed an exceptionally long period of peace in European history.[14]

Back to the Future visions rest on the realist interpretation of international politics, which sees competition and anarchy as basic elements. States compete for power and there are no given rules which regulate this competition. Anarchy reigns in this Hobbesian jungle, where everybody fights for survival against everybody else. The absence of central authority forces each state to rely on its own means to safeguard its existence.

While states compete for survival, they also form an insecure system. Constant preparation for war leads to a vicious cycle where the security of one decreases the security of others. A single state must arm to protect itself, but then others must in turn arm to protect themselves from the single state. According to a realist interpretation, this security dilemma continues despite the end of the Cold War.

What then prevents the system from destruction? States form a hierarchy because their power basis is not uniform. This hierarchy and constant competition leads to a balance of power which in principle deters from aggression and war. At best, a balance of power can evolve into a concert, which means that great powers agree on some common rules and in cooperation preserve the stability of the system.[15] The most renowned historical example of a concert of great powers is the Concert of Europe formed after the Napoleonic wars.

Realists view bipolarity as the most stable system. The balance of power between two poles is simple and predictable. Defections are not possible, as the system has only two poles and a commensurate balance of power can be easily achieved with nuclear weapons. However, it has been argued that the Cold War bipolarity was different from a conventional balance of power, as it rested on nuclear deterrence: It was irrelevant how many conventional or nuclear weapons each camp had if a sufficient (existential) nuclear deterrent guaranteed the basic stability of the system.

If one follows the logic of the Long Peace thesis--which sees the Cold War order as stable, perhaps even optimal, order--then the bipolar system can only be replaced by a more unstable, obviously less optimal, order. This leads to conclusions that European stability requires the retention of as many elements of bipolarity as possible. One example would be keeping Russia as a central element in the European system. Mearsheimer has even advocated nuclear proliferation as a key to maintaining European balance of power--a nuclear Germany would contribute to European stability by deterring aggression and preventing further military escalation by giving Germany a sense of "absolute" security via existential deterrence.[16]

Mearsheimer projects a future where great power rivalry in Europe leads to an unstable balance of power. Five or six great powers compete with each other--at best, forming ad hoc coalitions which provide a precarious stability, or, at worst, fighting constantly against each other. Back to the Future pessimism overemphasizes the unchanged structural determinants of European stability. History is thus a cyclical pattern, where the end of bipolarity will lead to a repeat of past bellicose behavior as the post-war social, economic and political transformation of Europe is unable to break the constraints of the anarchical state system.

With the end of the Cold War, End of History optimism promises constant harmony, Back to the Future pessimism perpetual war. The probable systemic outcome of the end of the Cold War in Europe lies some-where between these two extremes. The analytical spectrum offers a variety of predictions, the approximate center of which has been captured effectively by Jack Snyder and his concept of liberal institutionalism. This school of thought mediates well between Fukuyama's millennarian-ism and Mearsheimer's quasi-apocalyptic view.

The outcome of European politics after the Cold War is not predetermined. It is actually quite hard to even guess the shape of Europe in the years to come. However, it is essential to recognize that we are not dealing with events beyond our reach. Europe's future can be influenced. There is still room for politics.

Liberal institutionalism--to borrow Snyder's term--recognizes the potential risks inherent in a new non-bipolar system, but it also emphasizes that new important features exist which make Europe a qualitatively different place than it was in the period up to 1914. The balance of power between European states is still a central consideration, as are military force and conflicting national interests. In addition, however, Europe sports economic integration processes, transnational production mechanisms, and strengthening common political institutions.

Liberal institutionalism regards the binding of Eastern European states into common political institutions and economic interaction as central to European stability. Political institutions enhance mutual understanding by developing exchange of views. They also develop legitimate channels for solving mutual problems and mediating clashes of interest. Working backwards, it is not difficult to see why this theoretical construction emphasizes internal factors as determinants of international outcomes. Liberal theorists focus on the internal structure of states, economic links and international cooperation, and perhaps their best known thesis is that democracies do not fight each other.

The European Union is in the limelight of liberal institutionalist hopes. Economic and political integration has created deep and comprehensive mutual interdependence in Western Europe. This system functions as a guarantor of peace and stability, as the inevitable clash of national interests has been fruitfully channelled into mediating procedures deriving from common institutions.

The stability of Eastern Europe can be aided through a process of integration with the EU. As a first step, the European Union has extended such economic benefits to East European states as aid, assistance, and some limited trade concessions. Political interaction has also been initiated. A link to the European Union strengthens the internal political and economic structures of East European states and the prospect of eventual membership gives these states something to aim for, a hope of a better future. Trade, access to western markets and technology, and investment by West European companies form the basis for stable economic prosperity in Central and Eastern Europe; thus, EU enlargement eastwards should be considered as an investment, not as a bill.

Such was part of the thinking behind the Pact on Stability, also known as the Balladur Plan. Proposed by then French Premier Edouard Balladur in early 1993 to the European Union, it represented the first comprehensive solution to East European instability. By linking economic advantages and future EU membership to good internal and external political conduct on the part of the East European countries, EU countries could--in Balladur's argument--make good use of their own economic potential and appeal. The argument is a logical one, but, as with many arguments, it does not always stand the challenge of reality. While a number of (primarily bilateral) agreements have been signed under the Plan's umbrella wherein states have pledged to respect minority rights and international law, these generally serve only to reaffirm commitments entered into earlier and do nothing to effectively advance the integration of Europe or the political development of its eastern half.

Even where achievement can be demonstrated in the concrete way Balladur had hoped, liberal theory has been sorely tested. There was evidence of increased economic links and interdependence in Europe even before the First World War, yet that bloody "internecine" conflict occurred. Echoing a point first argued famously by economist and Nobel laureate Sir Norman Angell, John Mueller has posited that world wars do not rule out a qualitative transformation of world politics.[17] The cost of war, Mueller says, has outgrown its benefits, thus making it an irrational instrument of politics. Muller argues that nuclear deterrence has not been decisive in this development--war was an irrational instrument between industrial nations even before the invention of nuclear weapons. He sees the world wars as the results of anachronistic political systems in Germany, Japan and Italy which were out of touch with modern reality. One conclusion to be drawn from Mueller's thesis is that political leadership is crucial in maintaining stability--Europe needs political leaders who recognize the irrationality of war and who promote stable political systems which emphasize welfare instead of imperial glory.

According to Stephen van Evera, wars in 20th century Europe were due to internal factors, such as extreme nationalism and militarism within a rigid class-society.[18] Following this explanation, the end of bipolarity does not mean an increased risk of war. The structure of the international system is irrelevant if the internal nature of its components has changed. At the same time, war is irrational because production is increasingly based on information--production can no longer be acquired by conquest or coercion. The strengthening of democracy and classless society has removed support for militarism and hypernationalism. Van Evera, however, warns that the collapse of Soviet order in Eastern Europe can lead to instability by means of strengthening nationalism in the context of weak and fragile democracies.

To put it bluntly, End of History optimism argues that war is impossible. Back to the Future pessimism maintains that it is probable as countries disregard old ties or cooperation. According to liberal institutionalism, war between Western democracies--for example, France and Germany--is now impossible, but there are no similar guarantees for Eastern Europe. Thus the stability of that region and the integration of Russia into a regional framework are the main questions concerning European security for the immediate future.

Clearly, Europe is dominated by two prime processes, western integration and eastern disintegration. The West seeks internal strength by developing its integration further. Integration is also widening, assimilating new countries into its sphere of interaction. Moreover, although many believe the integration processes are laboring at a glacial pace, they are in fact moving very rapidly in a historical context. But at the same time, disintegration in the East is also proceeding apace, as economic and political reforms in the region fail to achieve their goals. European security seems to be a race between integration and disintegration.

As Peter Taylor has pointed out, geopolitical transitions contain different options vying for construction. For the purposes at hand, these options seem to be a united Europe with the EU as its core, a divided Europe with antagonistic Eastern and Western spheres, or a Europe of nation-states where integration recedes and gives way to great power rivalry on a continental scale.

* * * * *

A New World Order?

The new global code that emerged after the Cold War was eagerly defined by President George Bush as a New World Order, with the United States as a global leader. According to this view, the Cold War--the rivalry of two global superpowers--had ended in American victory. A similarity can be drawn between this New World Order and the expectations at the end of the Second World War in 1945, namely the "Grand Alliance" of winning powers would be able to produce a peaceful world without deep divisions.

The end of bipolarity can in principle lead to its replacement by unipolarity or multipolarity. Unipolarity would mean US leadership in world affairs. Multipolarity would mean the emergence of a system with more than two great powers, which would compete and--sometimes simultaneously--form alliances. The competition and cooperation among these great powers would lead to a more-or- less stable balance of power.

The emergence of one great power to challenge the United States seems unlikely for the time being.[19] Bipolarity has ended as a global code, but it can still be argued that some of its elements persist within the nuclear balance between the United States and Russia. Geopolitical transitions *are* seldom smooth, and if the previous bipolar order already contained some elements of the coming global constellation, it seems likely that future orders will keep fragments of bipolarity, for example, bipolar nuclear deterrence.

The Cold War was often analyzed as an ideological struggle between two conflicting "ways of life" or belief systems, the opposition of "Wilsonianism" and "Leninism." After the First World War, President Woodrow Wilson wanted to use US power to forge international relations in support of a more liberal order. President Wilson claimed that the US was a champion of the rights of mankind and a trustee for the peace of the world. Echoes of this position can be heard in US analyses on its new position in the post-Cold War order.

According to Samuel P. Huntington, the United States is the only nation on earth where democracy is an inalienable part of culture, European states may adopt democracy if it suits their interests, and Japan is fundamentally undemocratic. The world needs the United States' leadership as a guardian of universal values:

> The collapse of the Soviet Union leaves the United States as the only major
> power whose national identity is defined by a set of universal political and

economic values. For the United States these are liberty, democracy, equality, private property, and markets. In varying degrees, other major countries may from time to time support these values. Their identity, however, is not defined by these values, and hence they have far less commitment to them and less interest in promoting them than does the United States.[20]

Zbigniew Brzezinski espoused much of the same when he sees a contemporary US leadership of world politics based on values rather than economic or military power.[21]

This triumphant Wilsonianism vision, the New World Order, might have required US leadership, but it required international "supportership" as well. Thus the United Nations has a strong role in this unipolar vision, a global caucus. The war in the Persian Gulf was the first test for this grand new order. Old rivals--the United States and the Soviet Union--were united against a common enemy, an international thug who had transgressed the rules of the New World Order. The United States and the Soviet Union agreed that Iraq should be forced to retreat from Kuwait, the United Nations gave its blessing for the operation, and it could be said that the international community was united against a commonly-perceived enemy to world peace.

The interests of the "international commmunity" are not, however, always so clear cut. Consensus over the Kuwait crisis should not lead to the conclusion that similar ventures can be undertaken in the future. Saddam Hussein was the ideal enemy and oil-rich Kuwait a victim whose rescue was in the interests of all industrial nations. Future situations may not present such neat players and clean scenarios. The failed multinational military operation in Somalia was supposed to be the second chapter in global enforcement. The bogdown in the Former Yugoslavia has demonstrated the shortcomings of the New World Order and shown how national and even ethnic interests still prevail over universal values and norms.

Moreover, the war in the Persian Gulf will prove to be an exception rather than the model for other reasons. Bush's New World Order was really a sketch for a unipolar world order, or Pax Americana. Russia was relegated to a role of a regional power, and the United States alone assumed responsibility for global management. However, even if the international political situation after the Cold War calls for US leadership, the economic situation does not permit it.

On the whole, the arguments advocating the formation of a unipolar world order can be reduced to two primary theses, both of them flawed:

1) It is in the interests of the United States to keep its leading position in world affairs in order to safeguard it own interests.
2) US leadership is essential--and in the interests of all--in providing public goods, because it is the only country capable of acting as guardian of universal values, keeper of international order and guarantor of the liberal post-war economic system.

Unipolarity as a tool for US interests is likely to lead to conflicts with other powers. Differences of interest will force others to develop counter powers to US unilateralism, hastening the demise of unipolarity. Unipolarity as provider of public goods rests on the assumption that the United States will be able to forge policies acceptable to a majority and force compliance on the minority. A vision of the United States as a guardian of common or universal values is naive at best.

In the economic sphere, leadership and upkeep of the world trade and financial system has required sacrifices and resources from the leader. The provision of public goods involves costs, and agreement on common norms requires compromise, both of which are more concrete and visible--particularly when many see them as "debits"--than the less immediately demonstrable benefits accruing from leadership. Basically, the United States can no longer afford to be the leader of the world economic system. This has been in evidence since the collapse of the Bretton Woods system.

Even during the Cold War, that most "appropriate" of times, the presumption by the US that it was keeper of universal values invited suspicion by enemy and by ally alike; such an assertion was often perceived as a disguise for the advancement of unilateral US interests. Differences of interest between industrial nations regarding economic and political issues will force the United States to adapt to a more assertive Western Europe and Japan, which no longer so acutely need the US shield against a common foe.

The United States faces economic difficulties, even though its decline has often been exaggerated. The Gulf War could not have been waged without the US military, but the US could not have waged the war without Japanese and German financial assistance. A unipolar world order is likely to be fragile and cannot last. The gradual divergence of the interests of the allies will shape the new world order--whatever that term means--into something that bears little resemblance to the concept advocated by President Bush. It is for the mapping of the emerging new real world system that we must turn to an analysis of the current geopolitical transition and the options contained within it. The post-Cold War period "new orderism" is being replaced with a new complexity in the middle of the 1990s.

Notes

1. Noam Chomsky, *World Orders Old and New* (London: Pluto Press), 1994, p. 1; Kissinger, *Diplomacy*.

2. John Lewis Gaddis, *The United States and the End of the Cold War*, (New York: Oxford University Press), 1992.

3. See Geoffrey Parker, "Political Geography and Geopolitics" in *Contemporary International Relations: A Guide to Theory* (London: Pinter Publishers), 1994, pp. 170-181. Also Peter J. Taylor, "Geopolitical World Orders" in the book he edited, *Political Geography of the Twentieth Century: A Global Analysis* (London: Belhaven Press), 1993. The author is much indebted to Taylor's book for facts, analysis and, above all, inspiration.

4. For a thorough analysis of Mackinder's views, see Gerry Kearns, "Fin-de-Siècle Geopolitics: Mackinder, Hobson and Theories of Global Closure," in Taylor, (ed.), *Political Geography of the Twentieth Century.*

5. Taylor, "Geopolitical World Orders," p. 51.

6. Ibid.

7. Ibid., pp. 36-39

8. Lester Thurow, *Head to Head: The Coming Economic Battle Among Japan, Europe, and America* (New York: Warner Books), 1993, pp. 24-25.

9. Kennedy, *The Rise and Fall of the Great Powers.*

10. For a full treatment of how the CSCE's human rights dimensions in particular helped to ultimately speed up the demise of Russia's communist empire in Europe, see William Korey, *The Promises We Keep: Human Rights, the Helsinki Process, and American Foreign Policy* (New York: St. Martin's Press), 1993.

11. For a comprehensive exposition of the origins of containment and postwar US foreign policy, see Wilson Miscamble, *George F. Kennan and the Making of American Foreign Policy: 1947-1950* (Princeton: Princeton University Press), 1992.

12. Mearsheimer, "Back to the Future: Instability in Europe After the Cold War"; Fukuyama, "The End of History."

13. Jack Snyder, "Averting Anarchy in the New Europe," *International Security*, Number 4, 1990.

14. John Lewis Gaddis, "The Long Peace," *International Security*, Number 4, 1986.

15. Peter M.E. Volten, "Power Politics or International Organi zation in Central and Eastern Europe," in Jaap de Wilde and Hakan Wiberg, (eds.), *Organized Anarchy in Europe: The Role of States and Intergovernmental Organizations,* (London: I.B. Tauris), 1996, pp. 183-201.

16. Mearsheimer, "Back to the Future," pp. 5-56.

17. John Mueller, *Retreat from Doomsday: The Obsolescence of Major War* (New York: Basic Books), 1989.

18. Stephen van Evera, "Primed for Peace: Europe After the Cold War," *International Security,* Number 3, 1990.

19. Regarding the argument that the United States will maintain its preeminent position in world politics, see Joseph S. Nye, Jr., *Bound to Lead: The Changing Nature of American Power* (New York: Basic Books), 1990.

20. Samuel P. Huntington, *The International Herald Tribune,* 1993.

21. See, for example, his article, "The Premature Partnership," *Foreign Affairs* 73 (March/April 1994), pp. 67-82.

3

Emergence of the
New Economic System

"The GATT-Bretton Woods trading system is dead and a new system of quasi trading blocs employing managed trade will emerge."
--Lester Thurow

"The forecasts that a "trade war" will replace the Cold War could also turn out to be exaggerated. Still, as the rest of the world watches Europe's integration, it clearly is concerned by its meaning for others."
--Paul Kennedy

"The restructuring and expansion of multilateral institutions today is in this sense a long overdue 'debipolarization' of the international system and a process of building a multipolar system comprised of different layers of interlinked global, regional, subregional and bilateral agreements and regimes."
--Michael R. Lucas[1]

Geoeconomics

With respect to the economic foundations of the international system, the period around 1960 marked a turning point during the Cold War era. By that year, both Western Europe and Japan had recovered from the ravages of the Second World War, the communications revolution began to make itself keenly felt, and awareness of environmental questions and ecological issues began to heighten. The closed socialist societies remained outside these global-to-become processes, although in the 1970s China made a radical change by beginning its Long March to a market economy and opening its doors to the outside world. The Soviet Union and its satellites did not follow and they faced total collapse by the 1980s.

Subsequently, the end of the Cold War made such previously masked

conditions as the deterioration of nature and the environment, misery related to poverty, and the lack of human rights more visible in consequence. In general, one can list contradictory forces molding the late-
modern world after the Cold War as follows:

1. Globalization forces are mainly economic in nature. One characteristic of the globalization process is the separation of the symbol
   economy from the real economy since the Bretton Woods agreement was effectively sundered in 1971. As Pentti Malaska states,
   this divorce gave rise to the symbol economy and laissez-faire capitalism at the expense of the market economy system. Technology development, too, is a vital element in the globalization of the
   world economy.[2]
2. Integration forces are aiming basically at establishing protected free
   trade areas and are thus also to be regarded as economic in nature.
   Their mission is to enhance economic growth within their targeted
   realms to protect their businesses from outside competition. Such
   integration can be complemented by a politically motivated "hard"
   regionalism (like that of the European Union), but is usually much
   more a function of an economically motivated "soft" regionalism
   (such as lead to the creation of NAFTA).
3. The above-mentioned expansive/consolidative processes co-exist in
   time with fragmentative forces which are not easily separated from
   the nation-state. Their short-term aim is to break down the prevailing societal whole, and to create incoherence between societal
   and political aims. There are observers who claim, like Max Singer and Aaron Wildavsky, that the world is not progressing toward
   the "global village" but retreating into atavistic tribalism whose ug-
   liest--but by no means sole--expression is the "ethnic cleansing"
   witnessed in Bosnia.[3]

Altogether, the world has become more interdependent both for better
and for worse. I assume that for the period of the post-Cold War geopolitical transition, which may last until the years 2010-2020, the shift in
economic power centers will constitute the most important factor of global change. Therefore the forces of globalization and integration will
prevail over the more fundamentally *political* forces of fragmentation.
Consequently, this basic feature of development will facilitate the emergence of trading blocs and new political rivalry between the key blocs.

After the Second World War, a free trade-oriented world economic system emerged. Based officially on the General Agreement on Trade and Tariffs, it was effectively sponsored by the United States, which was central to this order. Basically, the US drafted and enforced the rules of the game, and the Americans also underwrote the costs of this system of exchange. The Soviets and their satellites never joined in or had any real influence on its structure, which thus followed the US prescriptions for over a generation.[4]

The collapse of the Cold War provided additional impetus to trade liberalization while at the same time unleashing tendencies that seriously threatened the free-trade regime. The breakthrough in the Uruguay Round of GATT negotiations and the contemporary unilateral liberalizing impulses in many national trade policies--particularly those of ex-communist and developing countries--have created momentum for the lowering of trade barriers. However, international free trade is at great risk. From a political point of view, as Western nations no longer face the commonly perceived threat of expansionist Soviet communism, they are under less pressure to act together and sacrifice economic self-interest for the sake of unity. At the same time, from an economic point of view, structural change of the world economy has sown new seeds of contention. Western economies face fierce competition from new producers and have difficulties in adjusting to an interdependent global economy whose center of gravity is shifting eastward with the ascent of China, the East Asian "tigers" and their followers. Western industrial states face adjustments which demand more of them than they have as yet been willing or able to give. At present, there is no official initiative under way to create a formal Asian trading system centered on China and Japan, whose exchanges escalate.

Geoeconomics and the Quality of Regionalism

Geopolitics is the study of the configuration of power in the international system. Geoeconomics is the study of economics from the point of view of its interaction with world politics and its consequences for a global distribution of forces.[5]

Geoeconomics is essentially that debate on the global economy which centers on trade blocs versus free trade and economic, "soft" regionalism versus politically-constructed "hard" regionalism.[6] According to some, the common advantages of free trade are likely to prevail as the GATT system gives way to a regime led by the new World Trade Organization. According to others, the world will be divided into competing trade blocs, one American, one European, and at least one East Asian.

The argument of this chapter is that "hard" trade blocs are, in fact, likely to emerge. However, one can partly accept also the argument of some, like Miles Kahler, that much of the regionalization that has occurred in the world economy is of the "soft" variety: the binding together of Hong Kong, China and Taiwan, or the investment of US and Mexican corporations across the Rio Grande before NAFTA was ratified. NAFTA is not viewed by the US administration as an antagonistic trading bloc formed to insulate America and to do battle with Europe and Japan but rather as a regional building-bloc in an increasingly globalized international economy. If NAFTA is a bloc, it rests, as Michael Lucas reasons, "on the notion that it must be open to non-American states and interact with the EU, Japan and the evolving framework of APEC, if the global economy is going to escape the trap of protectionism and thereby spawn a new era of post-Cold War prosperity."

Conventional economic theory on trade and international economics is underpinned by many unrealistic assumptions. For example, liberal theory on international trade emphasizes the common advantages of a more efficient distribution of production by means of free exchange, therefore suggesting universal advocacy for free trade by virtue of its common gains. This assumption holds true in only limited circumstances.

The critics of liberal trade theory point out how the gains from free trade are unevenly distributed in society--average gains do not reflect individual gains. Free trade in agricultural products, for example, benefits consumers and hurts previously-protected producers. However, the gains for the consumers are evenly spread in society, marginally benefiting a large number of consumers, while the disadvantages are borne by a concentrated group of producers. This has usually led to strong political mobilization of producers, bound to lose their jobs and markets with free trade, and weak mobilization of consumers with much less potent individual stakes at play. Governments are therefore usually much more vulnerable to pressures from producers than consumers.

The difference in logic between politics and economics is often characterized as the difference between "zero-sum" and "win-win" thinking. Politics is seen as a zero-sum game, where the advantage of one is translated directly into the disadvantage of the other; economics is presented as a case of win-win, or non-zero-sum, thinking, where gain does not necessarily imply a loss for others--on the contrary, free trade should foster gains for all participants.

According to conventional theory, politics emphasizes absolute gain, while economics emphasizes relative gain. What matters for power-oriented politicians is who gains more, that is, what the distribution of power and individual ranking in the international system is. What matters for economic actors is not power but wealth, and the precise distribution of wealth among actors is less important than the notion that everybody gains something.

It is sometimes argued that a more equal distribution of wealth in advanced economies shifts state behavior from power politics to matters of wealth and economics. In democracy, where a large segment of society has a stake in the economic well-being of the nation, politicians should concentrate on economics rather than power, seeking relative rather than absolute gains.

The assumption that economics is not a zero-sum game is flawed, at least in international economics. Conventional trade theory points out that if the distribution of production among states is allowed to happen naturally, by means of free trade, all gain from a more efficient pattern of production, which, ideally, will then take place in a location where the means are best placed and the end-product will be cheapest to obtain. A country well endowed in raw materials should concentrate on exploiting those raw materials, and a country endowed with industrial resources should concentrate in industry. This should, according to conventional trade theory, benefit all.[7]

It was pointed out earlier that this does not take account of the unequal distribution of gains within states. Another, perhaps more fundamental, objection exists as to the working of conventional trade theory: In reality, free trade not only affects relative gains but also affects absolute gains.

The assumption that free trade is beneficial to all participants is only true in a static analysis, when time is not taken into account. Free trade does produce an optimum distribution of production but, given the passage of time, the initial distribution of production leads to a pattern of winners and losers.

In a dynamic perspective, however, when time is taken into account, different sectors of the economy have substantially different rates of growth. The rate of growth--or the rise of productivity--within primary industries is usually quite low. In old--"sundown"--industries it is also low, while the rate of growth is usually highest in new technologies and modern services.

With free trade, different industries are located in different countries. In the long term, those endowed with high-growth industries benefit the most. A country which specializes in raw materials will see its economy grow slowly, a country which has a large number of receding industries grows slowly or shrinks, while one specialized in new industries--for example, state-of-the-art electronics, or information industries and services --will grow much more than the others.

The differential in the rate of growth does not need to be substantial to produce tremendous changes a decade or two. With a disadvantage-ous distribution of production, one country may be rocketed into the poorhouse and another into a rich man's club. The rise of East Asia, a relatively poor area as late as the 1960s that has developed into a new economic force of global dimension, is a case in point. China and Mex-ico may make the same transition. In reality--that is, in a dynamic, non-static setting--free trade affects both absolute and relative gains between states.

The difference between absolute and relative gains is accentuated due to a process known, in Susan Strange's piquant coinage, as the technolo-gical imperative.[8] In advanced industrial production, the next generation of products always contains more technology than the previous one, and these new technologies are becoming more and more expensive to fash-ion. Research and development costs have spiralled to new heights. At the same time, product-generations last for shorter and shorter periods. This means that larger R&D costs have to be recouped in a shorter time and has lead to a concentration of production in the hands of a few big producers. In the automobile industry, for example, rocketing R&D costs have lead to bigger and fewer producers. This iron law of consoli-dation works for most developed advanced industries.

The difference between relative and absolute gains attributable to free trade would not matter if there were enough advanced industries to go around for all major countries. However, concentration of production due to the technological imperative is bound to lead to some kind of pro-tectionist arrangements in the world economy.

All major industrialized regions are keen to have their share of ad-vanced production: cars certainly, but, more importantly, computers and information technologies as well. Otherwise, their rates of growth will stall and force them to accept a lower level of wealth. All want to have an advanced computer industry, the basic building block of this new economic chain, but this is impossible; only fewer and bigger producers can survive. North America and Europe fear that in most cases, if left to the markets, the winner will be Japan. This is bound to affect the future of free trade at some point.

While the case for the end of free trade and a regionalization of trade is strong, it is not watertight. The regionalization of the world economy would perhaps create more problems than it solves. One of the biggest obstacles to regionalization is perhaps its consequences for technological innovation. With only a regional entity as a market--rather than the global marketplace--advanced industries will either slow down their speed of innovation--to recoup higher costs from a smaller market--or raise prices. It should be emphasized that neither free trade nor regionalization are obvious choices. Much will depend on how advanced industrial nations choose to tackle the challenges of the world economy. Perhaps a closer look should be given to who decides on economic policy within leading industrial countries and regions.[9]

The Challenged American Economic Hegemony

"For all its economic and perhaps military decline, the United States remains the decisive actor in every type of balance and issue."

--Pierre Hassner

"The shape that regional institutions take in the future may well influence both the strategy of the United States and others within the international political economy."   --Miles Kahler[10]

All the key countries in the world system are compelled to follow an increasingly more complicated strategy to cope with the globalization of economy. In particular, a technological revolution that has not recognized state boundaries continues to put into question traditional realpolitik institutions and forms of political culture and communication inherited from the Cold War era and the 19th century. In the 1980s, the United States made a clear policy shift toward multilateral and regional institutions for safeguarding its economic interests. This followed at least partly from a perception that the country would or had already become one of the big "losers" of the international change as a result of its "imperial overstretch."[11]

After the Second World War, a new international economic system emerged under the tutelage of American strategic hegemony. Its pillars were the General Agreement on Trade and Tariffs (GATT) and the Bretton Woods monetary system, and the International Monetary Fund (IMF) acted as its central banker.

The underlying imperative of the post-war international economic system was the development of free trade. This would be realized by agreeing to common trade norms within GATT and a common payments and monetary system to facilitate trade. The United States took the responsibility for management of the entire system, giving economic concessions to others if it was necessary for the advancement of common good and offering its dollar, backed with gold, as the ultimate reserve currency.

Western currencies had a fixed exchange rate, which was an advantage for trade. Western governments held dollars as reserve currency, which the United States was committed to changing into gold, if needed. But the full faith and credit on which the international economic system functioned was "theologic" rather than fiduciary--so long as the US had the world's largest and most powerful economy, the specifics of foreign exchange and terms of trade were less important than the profile of the underwriter. And the system functioned as long as US economic leadership was credible, which is to say for nearly 25 years.

But with relative US economic decline the foundation of the monetary system crumbled. As a result of the Vietnam War and the contemporaneous "Great Society" programs of President Lyndon Johnson, the United States was forced into massive budget and trade deficits. This led to the breakdown of the Bretton Woods system. With US deficits, foreign governments began running sizable trade surpluses. With the subsequent amassing of very large reserves of dollars, the credibility of the US pledge to exchange them for gold at an agreed rate became dubious. To prevent a massive run on the dollar, President Nixon unilaterally declared the Bretton Woods monetary system finished in 1971. This was the end of fixed exchange rates and the beginning of new turbulence in the world economy. (In terms of the mid-1990s' dollar/yen suspense play and the unprecedented 80-odd yen per dollar, the fixed exchange rate of 360 yen per dollar of the Bretton Woods system gives a good perspective on international structural economic and monetary change since the early 1970s.)

Floating currencies meant that western governments had more room for economic action, as the discipline of fixed exchange rates no longer was a constraint. This opened a rift in western economic policies, which, compounded by the first "oil shock" (1973-74), revealed the structural weaknesses of advanced industrial economies. Their industries were energy-intensive, old and unproductive. All western economies were forced to embark on structural adjustments.

The United States resorted to protectionist measures, which may be a foretaste of future trade dispute resolution practices in Washington. The American car industry faced difficulties, because its products consumed much petrol. They were losing to Japanese competition, with its much more economical low-consumption models. The US government imposed so-called voluntary export restraints on Japanese producers, limiting the number of Japanese cars exported to the United States. These export restraints, however, in the long term worked to the detriment of US producers, because their Japanese competitors had an incentive to develop and export pricier models as their quotas were given in units. Quotas also froze the US shares of competing Japanese factories, thus making a lucrative domestic monopoly for Japanese exporters.[12]

With the end of exclusive American hegemony in the world economy and the collapse of the Bretton Woods monetary system in the early 1970s, multilateral management of the world economy became critically necessary. The first real attempt at such management took the form of regular meetings of the leadership of the major western industrialized states, otherwise known as the Group of Seven: Britain, France, Germany, Italy, the United States, Canada and Japan.

The basic idea behind G7 was that, as the United States could no longer afford to be the leader, decision making over economic affairs and ensuing costs would be assumed collectively. Macroeconomic management was the central goal of the enterprise.

The post-war leaders had learned their lesson from the inter-war period. The recession at the end of the 1920s in the United States had prompted protectionism--beggar-thy-neighbor, pass-the-buck policies-- which helped cause a deep recession in Europe when exports to America met with steep trade barriers. Recession in Europe in turn gave way to the rise of fascist regimes in the wake of massive unemployment and inflation. Post-World War II management of the world economy aimed at preventing this from happening again: Instead of protectionist policies that could force industrial nations into destabilizing recessions, relatively free trading and a system with shared norms would be followed.

Alongside waning American leadership, the growth of interdependence made collective management all the more critical. By definition, interdependence means the end of national unilateral economic measures--if one big western economy pursued policies in contradiction to the policies of another, they might well produce results that neither wanted. Thus with the "coin" of power increasingly economic in nature, an increasingly economic concert was necessary to maintain the balance.

The first G7 summit took place in Rambouillet, France, in 1977, and for several years thereafter the agenda concentrated on recession; the early years of G7 culminated in a very successful 1979 summit in Bonn, where the group agreed on common anti-recession measures. Since then, however, the results of the process have been far from successful.

During the 1980s, the main point of contention between the United States and its partners was the Americans' so-called double deficit. At the beginning of the decade, the dollar was very strong, reflecting both the American economic boom and high domestic interest rates due to a growing budget deficit. The American trade imbalance jumped to new levels, as demand in the United States was very strong due to massive tax cuts of the Reagan administration. These tax cuts also produced a massive budget deficit, which swallowed huge amounts of capital from international money markets.

Accordingly, the attention of G7 focused on currencies in the middle part of the decade. We can talk about a G7 dollar diplomacy, with the 1985 Plaza and 1987 Louvre accords as its hallmarks. These agreements signalled a high point in G7 cooperation, and the dollar was brought back to manageable levels. It should be noted, however, that much of this "dollar management" was performed by the central banks of the countries, which operate in varying degrees of independence from political authority.[13]

On most systemic issues, the G7 process has been marked by the development of two camps. One was led by the United States, advocate of a so-called locomotive approach. According to the US government, during western recessions the problem was underconsumption. Its prescribed solution was for G7 countries to boost demand and lower interest rates. The other camp centered on Germany and Japan, who favored a more structural approach. According to German and Japanese views, poor G7 economic performance was due to fierce competition from new producers--East Asia, for example--and the challenge would best be tackled by improving their economies rather than just inflating demand; inflation has alway been a greater sin than unemployment in their eyes.

For all the cooperation in currency issues in the mid-1980s, no agreement has really ever been reached to bridge the more fundamental differences on this basic analysis of the western economic situation. The United States has long thought that its partners have hindered global economic growth by focusing on domestic stability, while the partners of the United States have continually criticized US administrations for sacrificing long-term stable economic growth in favor of instant cures and immediate gratification.

By the mid-1990s, the dollar had once again become a main point of contention, which only betokened problems on bigger issues. The US government has seemed to want to have its way on all accounts--cut the trade deficit without cutting domestic demand. The G7 partners of the United States have advocated a reduction in US demand by increasing interest rates--less demand would mean fewer imports, thus an improving trade balance. The United States has resisted such stringent domestic measures for the most part and it has instead allowed the dollar to drift downward--reckoning that a weakened dollar will boost US exports. In the meantime, Germany and Japan have paid attention to inflation, and the economic policies of G7 governments have been contradictory, far from coordinated.

The G7 offers a perspective on how hard it is to achieve consensus on economic policy between western central governments. No agreement has existed on the basic analysis of economic problems and what to do about them. On the whole, the G7 experience points out to the difficulties of inter-governmental coordination on a global scale in the absence of a single political leader.

However, the multilateral institutions--GATT, G7, NAFTA, APEC--are the only realistic options for the United States and others to pursue their respective national interests in a regulated, common, and peaceful manner.[14] Like sports, the international economic game is one of structured competition with efficient and well-equipped systems of settling disputes, as Michael R. Lucas states.[15]

In the middle of the 1990s, the United States was still the only major industrial country that could revert to large-scale protectionism, "but the danger is slight," as Charles R. Carlisle reasons.[16] In fact, no country in the world embraces the belief in free markets and free trade to the degree that the US, Britain and other English-speaking democracies do. A number of regional trade arrangements in the Americas and in the Asia-Pacific area (as well as the further expansion of the European Union) have kept concerns regarding regional trade diversion very much alive. Yet an examination of the WTO's trade statistics suggests that this fear seems to be much exaggerated. Successive US administrations have understood that the growth of the American economy is due to free trade, not protectionism and isolationism.

The Ascent of Economic Blocs[17]

The end of the bipolar division has caused as much ambiguity in the international economic arena as it has in the diplomatic and security ones. As the western countries are no longer united by a common enemy, they may be more prone to disagreement on economic issues. More fundamentally, structural economic factors--more easily overlooked during the Cold War--may foster new, perhaps irreconcilable crises between western governments.

Despite the success of the Uruguay round of GATT, fundamental disagreements between advanced industrial economies exist. Bilateral negotiations, like the Japanese-American Structural Impediment Talks, often replace multilateral solutions as the place where real consessions are made. This may lead, as Lester Thurow observes, "to a trading bloc mentality."[18]

A consolidation of Western economies into economic blocs is on its way. In 1993, the three countries of North America concluded an agreement over a free trade area (NAFTA). Despite much internal opposition and questions about its future, Europe, or at least the bulk of its western part, is enforcing common policies. Japan is consolidating its economic grip over East Asia through direct investment, if not by institutional means. Trade wars between economic pan-regions may loom over a not-so-distant horizon.

North America is perhaps the weakest and most recent of these trade policy constructions. The agreement on free trade between Canada and the United States is quite recent. The association of Mexico into this North American area was a big step and may prove to be a way of integrating other Latin American economies into this trade bloc; Chile is actively lining up to be the next member. However, the policy coordination that is a fundamental aim of the European Union is not in sight in the Western Hemisphere; it is not even a theoretic possibility.[19]

Japanese companies have been increasingly investing in East Asia since the 1960s. This regional pattern of investment has produced a deep structure of de facto economic integration, a regional division of labor where Japan acts as a center. Japanese companies develop their most advanced products at their home "base" and also concentrate in Japan their product and technology improvements. To stay competitive with rising costs, however, they have long established production bases in less-developed countries. Newly industrialized countries, most prominently the East Asian "tigers" (South Korea, Taiwan, Hong Kong and Singapore), form a first line of junior economic partners. Thailand, Malaysia, Indonesia and the Philippines form a second chain of partners with even lower labor costs. A third line is still in its formative stages, with new interesting locations as Vietnam and, above all, China. Much of this "Japanese" production is aimed at export markets.

The Japanese economic sphere of influence in Asia forms a dynamic whole. Technology and investment flow from Japan to other Asian countries, which then export to Japan's customers. This has produced an unprecedented pattern of development, which also fosters local economies and has catapulted Asia to the forefront of global trade. Japan now trades more with its Asian partners than with the United States, in an integration process that many believe was triggered by the continuing economic integration of Europe and of North America.[20]

The formation of a Japanese-led Asian economic bloc has not produced common Asian institutions, as memories of a malign Japanese hegemony--the so-called Greater East Asian Co-prosperity Sphere, used as a fig leaf for brutal conquest by Japanese militarists during the Second World War--are too recent. However, economic links form an organic whole in Asia and, if needed, this may be a basis for some sort of a stronger political construction in the future if world trade is re-routed to a new path of protectionism and pan-regions. But, whether formalized through institutions or not, this soft integration is one of the most conspicuous examples of the world's current regionalizing tendencies.

Yet Europeans should face the fact that the policies of the European Union are perhaps the most decisive factors in the development of world trade. In GATT negotiations, the EU--often forced to act as the standard bearer for individual countries adopting hard-line policies (such as France did, for example, regarding the "onslaught" of American film exports)--was the biggest obstacle to successful agreement. NAFTA and Asian de facto integration are both in large part reactions to Western European developments. The expansion of an increasingly expansionist "Europe," with its Single Market, European Economic Area, and Economic and Monetary Union, is the largest worry in American and Asian minds concerning world trade, perhaps one of their few truly shared concerns. In large part, Europe has the responsibility for the future of world trade: Will that be strengthening free trade or gradually closing economic blocs?

What is the case for a future of economic blocs, or pan-regions? The North American Free Trade Area and the de facto Japanese economic space make no attempts at policy coordination. Where any coordination or harmonization has managed to develop, it is due to market pressures rather than political decisions. But if we focus on Europe, we find that the reasons are linked with the consequences of policy coordination, the decision-making structure and the previously-mentioned technological imperative.[21]

The European Union and, to a lesser extent its economic hang-around club, the European Economic Area, have embarked on far-reaching collective policy--all aspects of economic policy are to be coordinated, while such collateral areas as environmental protection are also to be harmonized to ensure the workings of the internal market. EU countries have a common commercial policy and a common agricultural policy, both of them issues of contention at global trade forums.

The consequences of policy coordination within a limited number of countries logically lead to a higher level of protection towards third parties. EU countries have, for example, agreed on a common minimum level of environmental protection to ensure that the Single Market will not lead to a degradation of environmental protection; otherwise, there would be a risk that some countries would be tempted to lower their environmental norms to attract industry by lower costs.

But such a policy simply shifts the potential problem outside the coordination area. What prevents outside producers from harming the environment outside the policy-area and then exporting at lower cost to the area which has higher environmental standards, thereby putting environmentally-conscious producers at a disadvantage? One alternative would be a global environmental policy. Then no producer could have a cost advantage that was detrimental to the environment. This is, however, hardly a realistic option. The 1992 Rio de Janeiro summit on the environment, which did not even emerge with an agreement on rhetoric--let alone policy and action--was a clear demonstration of the limited possibilities of global environmental policies.

The same logic applies to all kinds of policy coordination. If you enforce a guaranteed level of worker safety or worker rights within the boundaries of a given region, what prevents outsiders from competing at the costs of workers' rights or safety? It can be argued that policy harmonization does not lead to protectionism as the external situation of a given region does not matter for the policy-area in question: If West Europeans want to enjoy a high level of environmental protection, that is fine; if a certain country X does not care about its environment, that is its business and not the concern of others. This logic is, however, flawed. More and more problems have a global dimension. The environment, human rights and population growth are no longer--if they ever were--simply the internal affairs of states. Population growth will exhaust the necessary resources for mankind's survival. Environmental questions have a global dimension: The destruction of the rain forest has consequences everywhere. From a non-altruistic point of view, why would a given policy-region let others harm its economy and take away jobs by harming the environment?[22]

Policy coordination within Europe is likely to lead to more strict enforcement at its external borders. The logic that applies to environmental protection applies also to social rights, regulation of financial markets, consumer protection and any norms designed to change the behavior of markets. This is likely to be interpreted as protectionism and will prove to be a further, perhaps insurmountable, obstacle to a deepening of global free trade. European integration, especially its policy coordination aspects, presents a case for economic regionalization, a world of trade blocs.

A second factor, perhaps leading to further regionalization of world trade, is the composite nature of the European Union. NAFTA and the Japanese sphere make no attempts at purposeful policy coordination; the EU does, but it is still primarily a union of nation-states rather than a multinational entity. Consequently, the process of achieving consensus, that is, agreement on common norms, is often long, painstaking and complicated.[23]

The complicated and fragile decision making of the European Union is translated in the international arena into intractability at the negotiating table. The negotiating position of the EU has been reached after arduous work and a delicate balance between member-states. As a consequence, the EU can hardly move from its negotiating position at the negotiations, because flexibility could destroy the crucial interests of a member-state. It is easier to distribute benefits between member-countries than to agree that a member should take losses in favor of a third party. External partners usually become victims of internal agreement--such are the trade diversion aspects of customs unions and free trade areas.

The Uruguay round of GATT was a textbook example of the EU as an international partner. Consensus over EU targets was hammered out in the Council of Ministers among all member governments, while the EU Commissioner on External Trade represented the community at the negotiating table. However, the commissioner could hardly move from the agreed position and the GATT deal was effectively in the hands of the French government, which would not move from its views on agriculture and intellectual property.

With new members, the decision making of the EU will become even more rigid, making it an even more intractable international partner in trade. Only a deepening of the Union, meaning more majority voting by member-states for decision making and supranational executive powers for the European Commission, could make negotiating more easy. The EU has, however, failed to agree on the necessary reforms.

The Common Agricultural Policy (CAP) is a good example of both internal policy coordination and implications for external trade policy.[24] The CAP maintains prices far above international levels by means of a common external tariff and EU-wide price mechanisms. The CAP is far from optimal and is laden with many grave problems (more than one observer has noted that, a la the Holy Roman Empire, it is neither common nor agricultural nor a policy), yet its reform has proved elusive because alternative systems would provide new winners and losers. Therefore it remains, far from perfect but providing some level of advantage for everybody. The weaknesses of the CAP translate into rigidity as to the position of the EU on international agricultural trade, which amongst others, has prevented the exploitation of comprehensive advantages for third-world producers at the international level.

The third case for mounting protectionism is intimately linked with the aforementioned-technological imperative. Rising R&D costs and shorter product lifespan have led to a concentration of advanced industries. The EU has been losing its technological edge to United States and Japan. One of the basic motives for the Single Market was to restore European competitiveness by removing many of the micro-economic impediments to economic innovations.

If you compare the share of American, Japanese and European production in advanced industries, the picture is quite bleak from the European point of view. It is strong in declining industries and weak in the most advanced and information-intensive industries. However, Europe wants to have a significant share of advanced industry and the EU is fighting for it by political means. Continentalist economic and industrial policies have emphasized national champions and dirigisme, for the Europeans fear that a reliance on markets alone will doom them in the technological battle they are waging against the North Americans and the Japanese. To paraphrase Clausewitz, then, trade has become war by other means.[25]

Many EU countries have already enforced quotas on imports. For example, Japanese automotive imports have long been regulated to a fixed share in France and Italy to protect local producers. European producers have feared that with the restructuring of the automobile industry, Europe may be left with fewer or perhaps no major producers. The computer industry is another sector where major European companies, generally uncompetitive internationally, have become quite scarce.

So far, Western Europe has responded to its gradual decline with programs emphasizing improved European competitiveness rather than protection from outsiders. Education, research and technology, infrastructure improvements and a removal of internal rigidities are on the agenda to improve Europe's lot in global competition. These measures, however, take time to work and the patience of Europeans seems to be getting shorter with unprecedented levels on unemployment. The use of outright protectionist measures to shield European producers from outsiders is not unimaginable.

On the whole, the development of world trade into competing economic blocs depends much on the future policies of the European Union. Japanese policy is generally cautious and reactive, adapting to the global market and political climate. Elsewhere in Asia, and in North America as well, the consolidation of local trade blocs is usually seen as a desperate measure, to be resorted to in case of a crisis in international trade. While the building of a Fortress Europe is likely to provoke the formation of trade blocs, economic pan-regions, the formation of a world of antagonistic trade blocs is not yet a certainty. It is possible that regional policy coordination could be complemented at the international level, making regional policies compatible with global free trade. It is possible that the European Union will adopt a more efficient decision-making mechanism, thus making it a more flexible and sensible partner in international trade negotiations. It is also possible that Europe will regain a stable position within the global technological race.[26]

However, one can be sceptical. European policy coordination is unlikely to be supported by a satisfactory level of global policy coordination, and there is no international consensus on the environmental, social and other goals to be reached or how to reach them. The deepening of the union, making it an efficient actor in international politics, has definitively not advanced. The future of advanced European industries in the face of American and Japanese competition, remains also doubtful.

Besides European developments, economic disputes between the United States and Japan are also a contributing factor in global regionalization, the formation of trade blocs. The United States has been protesting for long about the persisting deficit with its trade with Japan. According to the US government, active measures should be taken to balance trade between the United States and Japan. The dollar/yen exchange rate has been a tool in the attempts to balance trade--a highly unsuccessful one, as Japan's trade surplus with the US has continued to grow virtually unabated despite the relatively low price of the dollar--and, therefore, of American-made goods--for the Japanese market. The United States has at times enforced quotas on Japanese exports and bilateral negotiations have taken place on reducing structural impediments to US imports in Japan; yet neither unilateral action, bilateral diplomacy, or seemingly favorable trade conditions have managed to smooth the course. The basic reason for the enduring trade deficit lies more in the different economic structure of Japan and the United States, rather than on Japanese unwillingness to import. Structural impediments to imports certainly exist in Japan, but they alone cannot account for the US trade deficit. Even if all structural impediments were removed, it can be argued that Japan can never afford to balance its trade with the United States.[27]

The United States is more of a continent than a state. It is well endowed in all factors of production, including raw materials. The picture is quite different across the Pacific; Japan's territory is rather small compared to the United States and it has almost no reserves of raw materials. Japan must import virtually all of its raw materials and energy.

The idea of balanced trade between industrial economies is nonsense from the Japanese point of view. Japan imports raw materials from developing countries and energy from oil producers. These countries, however, can never import as much from Japan as Japan imports from them, as their infrastructures are not suited to most Japanese high-tech exports. For structural reasons, then, Japan is bound to run a trade deficit with raw material and oil producers, a deficit which must be financed by a surplus in trade with other countries. In Japan's case, this surplus will be with the advanced industrial economies who demand Japan's industrial products. US demands for balanced trade with Japan are unacceptable. There seems to be no way for mutual compromise, as the United States and Japan view the trade deficit from fundamentally different perspectives.[28]

But perhaps the most fundamental reason for the regionalization of world trade is technological change. Advanced industries present viable opportunities for fewer and fewer producers. However, leading advanced industrial states all consider that they should have a fair share of those industries; their economic viability is at stake, because these coveted high-technology industries offer the fastest rates of growth. Due to rising R&D costs and shorter product-cycles, the competition for these industries is becoming fiercer.

In terms of the three principal economic blocs, Europe is lagging behind Japan and the United States and many fear that it is losing its technological edge. With its traditionally high-employment industries (such as automobiles) challenged by Japanese producers and with its future-related industries (such as computers) rapidly shrinking, the technological race may lead to one trade bloc--Europe--calling a stop to the game, which is to say that it will indulge in protectionism to shield its economic base.

The formation of trade blocs will lead to an alignment of less developed regions around the three advanced industrial blocs. NAFTA will lean on Latin America for markets and raw materials. Western Europe will eventually integrate Eastern Europe, Russia, Africa and parts of the Middle East into its economic sphere of influence. Japan will turn to East Asia, Australia, India, and China, although the latter may ultimate best the Japanese for economic leadership in the region.

A world of economic blocs may, however, prove to be a passing phase in history, perhaps out of tune with reality even when it is formed; economic and, above all, political reality is becoming much less focused on the trilateral world of economic blocs, because the center of gravity in economic and political affairs in shifting into new hands. The old masters are losing their grip. The weakest of the economic blocs--Japanese Asia--contains, or perhaps we should say borders, the largest political entity in the world, China. The Middle Kingdom is hardly likely to be subjugated into a junior economic partner to Japan. The geopolitical map may also change fundamentally, particularly in Southeast Asia, as a result of China's continuing economic growth. China may need to import 33 million tons of food a year 2020. As for oil, by 2010 the Chinese wil each year be wanting to import the equivalent of half of Saudi Arabia's total current production. They may try to get at least a substantial part of their oil demand met from nearby areas, such as the southeastern part of the China Sea. Undoubtedly, this will lead to increasing Chinese force projection in the region. Meanwhile, India is also a new force to be reckoned with. The Middle East will likewise probably escape the grip of any likely economic center. Neither can Russia be safely accounted into the camp of any world pan-region in the making. In simple terms, new world powers are rising during the relative decline of older ones, winners of the Cold War.[29]

The rise of new powers and the formation of a new international order is the key issue of the next century, with the rise of the successors of the current--and very transitory--tripartite world order of economic blocs.[30]

Notes

1. Thurow, *Head to Head*, 1993, p. 65; Kennedy, *Preparing for the Twenty-First Century*, p. 286; Michael R. Lucas, *The Clinton Administration and the Search for a Multilateral Economic Policy: The Role of GATT, NAFTA and APEC*, (unpublished manuscript: 1993), p. 3.

2. Pentti Malaska, "Progress, Nature, Technology," WFSF XIII World Conference Paper, Turku (Finland), August 28, 1993.

3. Many observers of international trade insist that "what is certain about the future is that the growing regionalization of trade...with the formation of competitive trade blocs will continue [and] so-called 'regional mercantilism' is on the horizon." See, e.g., Wayne Sandholtz, Michael Borrus, et al, *The Highest Stakes: The Economic Foundations of the New Security System* (New York: Oxford University Press), 1992, and also Singer and Wildavsky, *The Real World Order*.

4. See, e.g., Robert Gilpin, *The Political Economy of International Relations* (Princeton: Princeton University Press), 1987.

5. For a good analysis, see Robert O. Keohane and Joseph S. Nye, *Power and Interdependence: World Politics in Transition* (Boston: Little, Brown & Co.),

1989; also, Lucas, *The Clinton Administration.*

6. See Stephan Haggard and Beth A. Simmons, "Theories of International Regimes," *International Organization*, Summer 1987, pp. 491-517. About the regionalization of trade, *The Economist* (November 12, 1993) states that "a big trend in the world economy is towards 'regionalism' and the reassertion of economic geography."

7. See also Richard Rosecrance, *The Rise of the Trading State: Commerce and Conquest in the Modern World* (New York: Basic Books), 1985.

8. Susan Strange, *States and Markets* (London: Pinter Publishers), 1988.

9. For an interesting discussion on the relationship between economic forces and world politics, see Robert W. Cox, *Production, Power and World Order: Social Forces in the Making of History* (New York: Columbia University Press), 1987.

10. Kahler, "A World of Blocs," pp. 19-27; Pierre Hassner, "Europe and the Contradictions in American Policy," in Richard Rosecrance, (ed.), *America as an Ordinary Power* (Ithaca, NY: Cornell University Press), 1976, pp. 60-86.

11. During the Cold War, the decline of the United States as an economic power was very often cited, in particular in relation to the Soviet Union. See, for example, Kennedy, *The Rise and Fall of the Great Powers*, pp. 514-535. The current book treats a number of contemporary powers, reflecting the emergence of multipolarity.

12. There is no unanimity on whether the United States is in "decline" economically. There are observers who insist that the 21st century will be as American as the 20th has been. For an introduction to this debate, see John G. Ikenberry, "Rethinking the Origins of American Hegemony," *Political Science Quarterly*, Fall 1989, pp. 375-400.

13. On the history of the G7, see John G. Ikenberry, "Salvaging the G7," *Foreign Affairs*, Spring 1993, pp. 132-139.

14. For the argument that the United States and Japan should establish a new partnership to promote a multilateral trading system, see C. Michael Aho, "America and the Pacific Century: Trade Conflict and Cooperation?" *International Affairs*, Vol. 69/1, (1993). I confine the use of "hegemony" to America's role in the world political economy, recognizing, however, that there is a close interaction between economic and political dominance. As Herman Schwartz puts it in his 1994 *States Versus Markets* (New York: St. Martin's Press): "Hegemonic capacity has a military side as well as an economic one. In order to function, businesses need security and stability--the assurance that goods shipped will arrive, that contracts will be enforced, and that the world in general is predictable." The possible economic and social problems of the United States are related to the emerging polarization (rich and poor) of that country. If this trend continues, the US will face huge problems in the 21st century. This question, however, is beyond the scope of this book. I refer readers to the work of

Edward N. Wolff, particularly his *Top Heavy: A Study of Increasing Inequality of Wealth in America* (New York: New Press), 1995.

15. Lucas, *The Clinton Administration.*

16. Charles R. Carlisle, "Is the World Ready for Free Trade?" *Foreign Affairs,* Volume 75, Number 6, pp. 113-128.

17. For a further discussion of economic blocs see Robert Z. Aliber, "Three Scenarios for the World Economy," *Ethics & International Affairs,* Vol. 2, 1988; Joan Edelman Spero, *The Politics of International Economic Relations,* (fourth ed.), (New York: St. Martin's Press), 1990; Jeffrey J. Schott, *The Uruguay Round: An Assessment,* (Washington, DC: Institute for International Economics), 1994.

18. Thurow, *Head to Head,* p. 63.

19. On the other hand, for a discussion of tacit cooperation without centralized political order, see Stephen D. Krasner, *International Regimes* (Ithaca, NY: Cornell University Press), 1984; also, Oran Young, *International Cooperation: Building Regimes upon Natural Resources and the Environment* (Ithaca, NY: Cornell University Press), 1989.

20. See, e.g., Walter Russell Mead, "On the Road to Ruin: Winning the Cold War, Losing Economic Peace," *Harpers,* March 1990, pp. 9-64. In 1992, Japan sold US$12 billion and bought US$17 billion worth of Chinese goods, and Japan, Hong Kong and Taiwan were responsible for 85% of the US$11 billion in foreign investment in China, which rose 160% over the previous year. See Tim Weiner, "CIA Says Chinese Economy Rivals Japan's," *The New York Times,* August 1, 1993.

21. See the analysis about emerging trading blocs from the point of view of a "united Asia" versus the United States and Europe in Yoichi Funabashi, "The Asianization of Asia," *Foreign Affairs,* November/December 1993, pp. 75-82.

22. See, e.g., Kennedy, *Preparing for the Twenty-First Century,* pp. 95-121.

23. See also Kenneth Oye, *Cooperation Under Anarchy* (Princeton: Princeton University Press), 1985.

24. The Common Agricultural Policy (CAP) was launched in 1966. To outsiders, the CAP was seen as a protectionist tariff wall designed to maintain politically acceptable but artificially high prices for farm products produced within the then EEC. Its "egregiously mercantilist" program of internal supports and import levies curtailed foreign competition and stimulated large surpluses that were then dumped on the world market through export subsidies. See Don Babi, "General Agreement on Tariffs and Trade," in Joe Krieger (ed.), *The Oxford Companion to Politics of the World* (New York: Oxford University Press), 1993, p.344. In fact, the CAP effectively restricted US agricultural exports to the then EEC (which by the 1960s had become a principal trading partner of the United States).

25. In this context, see also Robert O. Keohane, *After Hegemony: Cooperation and Discord in the World Political Economy* (Princeton: Princeton University Press), 1984.

26. See, for example, Vincent Cable, "Key Trends in the European Economy and Future," in Hugh Miall (ed.), *Redefining Europe: New Patterns of Conflict and Cooperation* (London: Pinter Publishers), 1994, pp. 89-112.

27. See, e.g., Frank Gibney, "Creating a Pacific Community," *Foreign Affairs,* November/December 1993, pp. 20-25.

28. See "Tomorrow's Japan," *The Economist,* July 13, 1996.

29. See, for example, Kent E. Calder, *Asia's Deadly Triangle: How Arms, Energy and Growth Threaten to Destabilize Asia* (London: Nicholas Publishing), 1996.

30. For a fundamental analysis of international cooperation, see Robert Axelrod, *The Evolution of Cooperation* (New York: Basic Books), 1984.

4

New Geopolitical Actors
On the Rise

"...the geopolitical economic (geopolinomic) world order of the twenty-first century will be quite unlike the order of the mid-twentieth century....Geopolitics will not only be funded by a world economy, it will increasingly be obliged to serve it."

--Stuart Corbridge

"Conceivably, a new multipolar distribution of power could culminate in a renewed struggle for supremacy that could end the longest period of great-power peace in modern history."

--Charles W. Kegley Jr. & Gregory Raymond

"Nation states remain the principal actors in world affairs. The most important groupings of states, however, are no longer the three blocs of the Cold War, but rather the world's seven or eight major civilizations."

--Samuel Huntington

"Culture serves authority, and ultimately the national state, not because it represses and coerces but because it is affirmative, positive, and persuasive."

--Edward Said[1]

The previous chapter concentrated on the dynamics of the international economy. The latter's transformation is not just quantitative, but qualitative as well; it is not solely a question of more trade and intra-state economic relations, but also an unprecedented scale of transnational production and global markets which transcend national borders and political systems.

With the transformation of the international economy, one may ask if international politics is consequently transformed and its logic of operation different. This question is crucial when we assess the future of the international system.

Competing Predictions

There are schools of thought that emphasize the subjugation of economics to politics: In the last resort, what counts is the possession of military force, as civilian economic structures are naked before military aggression. The opposing school of thought points out the autonomy of transnational economic actors from territorial political entities: A multinational corporation can freely choose where to set up production, it is not a hostage to any state. Likewise, global financial markets can topple governments, which are seemingly powerless in the face of these new transnational economic actors and systems.

Yet states, even if they have to operate in a new international economic environment, still value power--the power which allows them to influence events and protect their existence--and security is a central consideration. The debate about which comes first--economics or politics--may be fruitless. It is apparent that global economic forces coexist with political systems in separate spheres of action and logic which cut across each other, and that a fairly large space exists where politics and economics interact. Geopolitics still has a role to play in the modern age of transnational corporations and global markets. And like politics, economics will have to adjust to a new international order.

Despite the profound changes of the international system, the basic framework has remained for two geostrategic realms--the trade-dependent maritime world and the Eurasian continental world. Of the five or six major power centers, however, only one is currently both a military and economic colossus: the United States. Two have been militarily strong but economically weak (Russia and China), while two are dominant economic forces that lack commensurate military capacity (Japan and the European Union). Since the end of the Cold War, these realities have been in the process of constant change. New strategic coalitions may emerge between the continental and maritime powers. Will any of these new coalitions gain hegemony in the system?[2]

According to Samuel P. Huntington, the world is bound to organize into competing cultures, into a "clash of civilizations."[3] In Huntington's view, the collapse of ideology will be replaced by another intellectual construction, culture. With the end of ideological rivalry, the world will organize itself into seven macro-cultural regions: Western, Orthodox, Muslim, Hindu, Confucian, African, and Latin American.

In Huntington's view, the rivalry--and conflict--among these cultural spheres will be fierce. These cultures represent fundamentally different and antagonistic ways of conceptualizing basic values and of seeing the world. In his view, for example, the world of a Muslim excludes that of a westerner. Huntington sees telltale symptoms of the clash of civilization in contemporary politics. When China sells arms to Iran, it is the proof of a collusion between Muslim and Confucian cultures against the western sphere. When Russia supports Serbia, it is a symptom of the consolidation of Orthodox culture.

Huntington challenges the theorists of international relations (IR) by oversimplifying the whole research subject. Theorists from a variety of different perspectives broadly agree that the international system came into being through the expansion of the West European state-system of the 17th century. Most scholars agree also that the international system emerged as a result of European power and the subsequent subordination of other cultures, and that, in significant respects, the international system continues to reproduce European culture forms in the process of reproducing itself. In brief, European culture is the first to have acquired the power to make itself a world system. In order to follow Huntington's considerations, then, one can ask whether it is possible for a culturally unipolar world system to be replaced with a multipolar system of six or seven cultural entities.[4]

Huntington fails to understand the internal dynamics of different cultural spheres and their fundamental pluralism. In his analysis, Muslim fundamentalism is, for example, depicted as a primarily anti-western and anti-American movement, radicalizing Islamic countries into a common anti-western international actor. Muslim fundamentalism is, however, usually a movement with domestic motives and dynamics. It is essentially a reaction to the modernization of Islamic countries, as traditionalist segments of society mobilize against changes that threaten their position.

Undoubtedly, civilizations and cultures will gain importance in the process which is "structurizing" the post-Cold War international system as a whole. Michael Mann once stressed that the international system results from the interaction of four social bases--economic, ideological, political and military. Mann castigated the discipline of international relations for its failure to analyze the integration between the national and the international. He argued that the concepts of international space held by what he describes as the two main traditions of IR are limited. In his view, realism is restricted to a view of the international system as structured by the interest of states; by contrast, "interdependence" concentrates on the mutuality of economic interests. In Mann's view, both these positions are limited, because the international arena is clearly some kind of combination of both (as well as other) phenomena, "and both impact greatly upon domestic societies, states and economies."[5]

In different historical epochs, different sources of power may be determining, alone or in combination. During the 18th century, economic and military sources of power were predominant, whilst in the 19th century this changes to a combination of the economic and political. During the end of the 20th century and beginning of the 21st century, a shift from a military-political combination of "hard" power to a a knowledge-economic-political combination of "soft" power has been obvious. Joseph S. Nye, Jr. and William A. Owens stress that the new political and technological landscape is ready-made for the United States to capitalize on its formidable "soft" power tools to project the appeal of its ideals, ideology, culture, economic model, and social and political institutions, and to take advantage of its international and telecommunications networks. In fact, the US increasingly provides this cultural "umbrella"--an American civilization--for the rest of the world. The question is whether this process, if it continues without major breaks, is dismantling the civilizations with different cultural identities.[6]

From another point of view, what really matters is that the US restores its status as number one by substituting "geoeconomic conflict" with states that do not trade "fairly" (such as Japan and the European Union) for the geopolitical conflict of the Cold War. This book tries to make the argument, which is to a large extent in compliance with the theories of Michael Mann, that "the international arena" consists of "multi-power-actor civilizations" and may lead to "empires of domination." I assume that there will be both democratic and authoritarian trading blocs in the international arena, which is the rub. If even one of the six or seven key players is a non-democratic power, a real possibility of geopolitical conflict exists. At the end of the 20th century, the international system was heading toward multi-power-actor centers which I call "trading blocs" because their organizing principles center on a "hardening regionalism" in terms of economic cooperation and integration.[7]

This book tries to make the argument that, at the system level, a process toward a global economic and political space is gaining ground because of the end of the Cold War and the globalization of financial markets, market economies and technological innovation. The question is simply whether the international system is becoming more cooperative and less anarchic as a result. Is a global "value space" emerging too? From a theoretical point of view, is power politics, then, going to be replaced with institutionalism and cooperation? I will pay special attention to a constructivist analysis of cooperation which concentrates on how the expectations produced by behavior affect identities. The post-Cold War period of the disappearance of old threat perceptions provides a starting point for discussion of the transformation of identity through "an evolution of cooperation." As Alexander Wendt states,

> ...the process of creating institutions is one of internalizing new understandings of self and other, of acquiring new role identities, not just of creating external constraints on the behavior of exogenously constituted actors....This will tend to transform a positive interdependence of outcome into a positive interdependence of utilities or collective interest organized around the norms in question.[8]

The argument is that increasing interaction at the systemic level--e.g., between trading partners and between trading blocs--changes state identities and interests. Are the actors able to construct social reality accordingly? From the international system point of view (whether it will be co-operative, conflictual or even dangerous), the question will be who (e.g., the US) will ally with whom (China or Europe or Russia) against whom (could it be Japan and the US against China)? What kinds of power coalitions will emerge?

The end of the Cold War witnessed the dismantling of the bipolar balance of power. The expectations after the collapse of the Berlin Wall were first ecstatic, with predictions of the birth of a new global political system based on agreement and harmony. These hopes soon vanished, however, as new conflicts emerged and old ones resurfaced. The international system became unstable again. In fact, it had not been "stable" to begin with.

The bipolar division of power kept western powers on the same side, united under a common banner. The international economy is a political system based on political agreements and norms, the so-called rules of the game. With the end of the Cold War, disagreement among advanced western economies is likely to lead to a degeneration of free trade, and the international economy will be based on three competing pan-regions: North America, Europe and East Asia (the latter led by Japan for the immediate future). This trilateral world of economic blocs is, however, only an intermediate phase. New power centers are bound to emerge and international rivalry will not be limited to the economic sphere. Power politics will make a comeback, and the new world system will be a political construction, with economics once again playing a subordinate role. New political and military blocs will emerge accordingly.

The international system is characterized by different modes of action, which form a scale: cooperation--competition--rivalry--conflict. The problem of the international community is how to keep international relations at the level of cooperation, or, at worst, competition, and prevent inter-state relations from degenerating into rivalry and conflict.

The tripartite world order of the United States, Western Europe and Japan will be challenged by China, Russia and the Middle East. The next passages focus on the challengers of the western system of economic blocs and draw a sketch of the coming world order.

The Pacific Century:
Rivalry or Cooperation Between China and Japan?

"The myth of a 'Pacific Rim Community' cannot compete with the alliance of interest and culture in various forms of pan-Asianism."

--Michael Lind

"Now, though Confucianism is gradually coming back to China, it cannot be compared to the increasingly forceful influence of Western culture...in the last 20 years....Nowhere in China is there a group or political faction that could be likened to the extreme nationalists of Russia or Europe."

--Liu Binyan

"Despite the end of the Cold War--perhaps because of it--the nations of East and Southeast Asia are engaged in accelerating arms races with significant implications for regional and international security."

--Michael T. Klare[9]

The 21st century has usually been described as the Pacific century, a Japanese era. Most certainly, the next century will feature an international system that for the first time has the Pacific region as its primordial core and actor. For the 21st century, the key security in Asia will be the emerging new relationship between China and Japan. James Fallows speaks about a specifically Asian system emerging, which combines mercantilism with authoritarian policies.[10] Although the common perception of this oriental combination is associated with the emerging economies of non-communist East Asia, it is certainly well exemplifed by Dengist China. In my view, this Chinese order will be the chief characteristic of the Asian century.

Although Japan has been the West's partner since the end of the Second World War, it belongs geopolitically--at least partly--to the "Asian community," irrespective of whether the lattter is a maritime or continental power. Japan may have a real geocultural temptation toward "pan-Asianism" and purely an economic interest in "Pacific Rim thought." In the future, the test will lie just here: Will Japan's geocultural interests supersede its geoeconomic (geopolinomic) ones?[11]

The strategic map of the world will be most strongly influenced by the growth of Asia and its increasing demand for oil and food in the world markets. China in particular will grow more dependent on the Middle East, the world's lowest-cost source of oil, with the volume of petroleum passing eastward through the Strait of Malacca likely to triple before 2010. In strategic terms, this will lead to the strengthening of the new linkage between China, as a net oil importer since 1993, and the Persian Gulf states, particularly Iran. This development may increase tension between China and Japan (in regards Iran, it will certainly increase tension between China and the West, particularly the United States).

Concerns have also been expressed about the emerging shortage of food as a result of China's need for grain imports. Lester R. Brown has predicted that by the year 2030, China's imports of food will far outstrip the spare production capacity of exporting nations. International food prices will skyrocket, imperiling consumers in poorer importing countries. First of all, China's international behavior will be influenced by this strategic dependency on foreign countries. This dilemma may not necessarily be solved by peaceful means alone.[12]

I disagree with those who, like Paul Krugman and Lester Thurow, who speak about "the myth of Asia's Miracle" and claim that China will not have a big impact on the world economy in the the first half of the 21st century.[13] In the 1960s, American futurologist Herman Kahn foresaw a century of prosperity marked by ever-tighter integration between the United States and what we call today "the Pacific Rim." Kahn did not foresee the rise of China, but if added to the overall prospect of "Asia's miracle," we are dealing with the most important strategic change in the power relations among the world's key actors since the end of the Second World War, let alone the end of the Cold War. It should be noted in this context that both China and Japan drive mercantilist policies aimed at running up surpluses, not at generating mutually beneficial trade.[14]

The assumption of a coming Japanese era has usually been extrapolated from its immense economic power and dynamism. Japan, the economic equivalent of two Germanys in the Pacific, is the first country in history to produce a $100 billion trade surplus. It is the world leader in new technology. Japan's industry has adequately responded to all challenges, making it stronger with every crisis. The oil shocks and the strong yen have only forced the Japanese economy to evolve into an even more dynamic and competitive force.

Continuing Japanese economic prowess and its position as a first-class civilian power, however, depend on certain international political factors: open trade and self-restraint in its strategic capabilities. Japan needs an open international economic environment to thrive. Western markets are necessary for its prosperity, for neither its domestic customers or those in its rapidly growing Asian markets can replace western clients. Thus, with a regionalization of the international economy, Japan is bound to be one of the big losers. Yet sympathy would be misplaced: Japan had a trade surplus of $53.6 billion with the rest of Asia during 1993. A predictable course might be a turn in favor of becoming more an integrated part of "Asian regionalism." Japan is siding increasingly with Asia's growing irritation with the American tendency to deliver sermons on human rights, free trade, multilateral diplomacy, democracy, and virtually anything else, regardless of the rather tacky record of the United States (and Europe) in many of these areas.[15]

The weakness in Japan's position is revealed by an analysis of the security of the Pacific basin, which has rested on US protection. The United States is the world's leading naval power. Its Pacific fleet protects Japan's vital sea routes and keeps China's military power in check. If competition between Japan and the United States leads to rivalry, with the regionalization of world trade and collateral political damage, Japan's vital sea routes would be left unprotected, its access to markets, energy and raw materials vulnerable.[16]

A reconfiguration of Pacific security by means of a withdrawal of US protection from Japan would mean a need for Japan to develop a strategic naval capability, a world-class blue water navy capable of protecting sealanes leading to the Indian Ocean. Japanese military measures do seem to foreshadow a more active naval presence in the Pacific, such as development of a new long-range capability to protect vessels from submarines--a basic element for Japan's viability as an insular power. Yet domestically, let alone internationally, an enhanced Japanese military posture is extremely controversial. Its US-drafted constitution limits the role and size of the armed forces to defensive purposes very strictly defined geographically, and many Japanese have grown comfortable with such constraints--witness the political difficulties successive Japanese governments had in the 1980s and 1990s to permit Japanese armed forces' participation in international operations even in support functions. And the financial burdens entailed by a higher military profile would not be easily shouldered: irrespective of any debate as to whether Japan's share of national resources consumed by the defense sector is very small by western standards, any increase would face severe opposition given the economic malaise affecting the country in the mid-1990s.[17]

But even if domestic opinion came around in favor of a growing martial capacity, the reinvigoration of Japan's military presence in the Pacific would run into a big obstacle: China. Beijing is not likely to accept Japanese naval or strategic assertiveness. Japanese control of vital sea lanes leading to the Malacca Straits would run along China's eastern coast and would exacerbate the already tense area around the Spratly Islands, where the Chinese are already exerting claims in the face of regional opposition. Moreover, China would naturally be unwilling to accept Japan as a nuclear power.[18]

Japan is a first-class economic actor, but on a strategic plane it can never surpass China. Japan has 120 million inhabitants, China 1.2 billion. China's per capita gross domestic product has to be only 10% of Japan's to be at par. The World Bank estimates that the Chinese economy was in 1994 about 40% as large as that of the United States; if China can continue to grow at a 10% annual rate, by the year 2010 its economy will be one-third larger than that of the United States. Even if the growth rate rate slows to more sustainable figures, a dramatic strategic shift of gravity in world politics, perhaps a more profound one than was confirmed at the end of the Second World War, is in store.[19]

Even without China's rapid economic growth, Japan could not translate its immense wealth into a bigger military capability than the Middle Kingdom's. Japan has other critical strategic disadvantages: It is a vulnerable insular nation, dependent on imports for energy and raw materials, and on foreign markets for its prosperity. This is a rather fragile situation, easily disturbed by any conflict--hot or cold. Thus if Japan attempts or is forced to assume a new military role due to a withdrawal of US protection, the best situation it can hope for is a Cold War with China, something it can never win.

Japan's only viable option therefore is to choose strategic and military restraint. It should either try to keep the United States as its protector or it should remain neutral in a possible Chinese-American Pacific balance of forces, a civilian power in an uncivil world.

The turning point in China's recent history was the accession to power of Deng Xiaoping, who brought with him major economic reforms. Deng transformed China from a backward and isolationist hermit kingdom into a powerful political actor and economy. Reforms have unleashed unprecedented economic potential and have produced the phenomenal double-digit growth figures. Given China's size, this growth marks a tectonic shift in world politics and its center of gravity.[20]

The consequences of Chinese economic reform and transformation have been to a large extent naively interpreted in the West. Many argue that, with economic reforms, China is on the road to democracy and decentralized command. This is not the case. A specifically "Asian system" has begun to emerge, based on a combination of mercantilism and authoritarian policies. Economic reform is a political tool in the hands of the Chinese leadership and its boundaries are well enforced. The Tiananmen Square massacre of 1989 gave a clear signal of Chinese priorities: economic freedoms will not be allowed to compromise China's centralized political system. With a keen sense of history, China's leadership regards centralized political control as a vital requirement for the country's power and standing in the international system. Thus economic reforms are meant to both keep the Chinese people fed--and therefore responsive to authority--and to expand the resources available to China as it seeks a leading position on the world stage.[21]

Yet while China's rise to political pre-eminence in world politics is very likely, there are distinct possibilities that this may not happen after all.[22] Using Peter Taylor's argument that geopolitical transitions are tran sitory phases containing many potential outcomes, the future of central state control is the most important indicator to be watched.

While the ultimate outcome of the struggle for China's economic soul may not necessarily mirror that for its political one, the range of possibilities is similarly broad. Given the current composition of the Politburo, it is conceivable that over the next several years an anti-reformist strain could dominate economic thinking, increasing the mercantilist aspects components of Chinese economic growth and heavily emphasizing the centralization that is still evident in China (free traders and liberals should note that Chinese policy, otherwise a study in ambiguity and ambivalence, is uncharacteristically clear on one issue: Beijing does not now seek, and has never sought, a market economy).[23]

On the other hand, it remains possible that this same Politburo could, if only by default, preside over a continued gradual and incrementally-paced decentralizing such has been ongoing economically since Deng consolidated his power in the late 1970s. The glacial pace of this reform was only partially a reflection of political reality (that is to say, a testing of the *political* limits attendant to the reform process); the Chinese authorities were also always conscious of trying to calculate the precise balance between decentralization and control that would unleash the country's economic potential without encumbering the *economic* costs (inflation, unemployment, and the like) that central planning had theoretically rendered obsolete.

In my view, an interesting--and plausible--scenario invokes patterns characteristic of early 20th century Chinese history. Soon after Sun Yat-sen's revolution of 1912, the China freed from the imperial yoke broke up and warlords came to rule over various regions of the country. The writ of central government did not hold in these fiefdoms. More than 70 years later, it is possible, despite the centralizing policy of the Chinese state, that economic reforms will lead to the autonomy of at least several provinces. This is already happening. If dynamic economic regions like Guangzhou and others escape from Beijing's grip, then we may even face a future where the current orientation of the world system of economic blocs will prove to be durable. Where China as a whole is much too large to be assimilated into a Japanese-oriented economic and political sphere, the various regions that make up the country might not be and could opt to follow Tokyo's lead rather than Beijing's.

This economically-prompted centrificality, which would have repercussions far beyond China, will, however, be difficult to reconcile with a

new and more assertive China in the military sphere. China is geopolitically dominant in East Asia, but its reach extends also to the heartland
(Russia), South Asia, and offshore Asia. As Saul B. Cohen states, China
"is in balance with the heartland but underbalanced with offshore
Asia."[24] The People's Liberation Army (PLA) has abandoned its reliance
on large manpower and has opted for a more professional and technol-
ogy-oriented approach, which may have been hastened by the lessons of
the Gulf War. It is very revealing of the country's priorities that the
PLA is actually in the forefront in profiting from economic reforms, running hotels, export enterprises, a large arms industry and technology ven-
tures--collecting cash and developing weapons for its own modernization. From the organization's point of view, economic reforms are not
intended to change the Chinese system but instead to assist and strengthen it.

Up to the 1980s, the PLA was a land army, with an obsolete air force
and an antiquated brown water navy suitable only for coastal patrol.
This has changed rapidly. The air force has embarked on a modernization program, starting with the purchase of SU-27 aircraft from cash-
poor Russia (with possible subsequent manufacturing in China). The
Chinese have even held talks with Ukraine about purchasing Soviet-era
aircraft carriers, now redundant on the Black Sea, in the hope of upgrading their maritime capacity towards a large blue-water navy with major
force projection capability.

China's strategic ambitions have a promising testing ground in the
Spratly Islands archipelago off the coast of Vietnam, a collection of mi-
ni-islands and isolated rocks. It has, however, great importance due to
oil deposits and a strategic location on the sea route from Japan to
Singapore, Japan's lifeline. All coastal states have laid claims on the is-
lands--Vietnam, the Philippines, Malaysia and China. Both China and
Vietnam have a symbolic military presence on major rocks. China has
developed a new military capability for enforcing its claims. China's
new SU-27 fighter aircraft can patrol the area from mainland China and
the upgraded navy is capable of operating in the vicinity. The rivalry
over the Spratlys shows China's new ambitions and is bound to lead to
China's permanent presence in the South China Sea, once the sole pre-
rogative of the US Pacific Fleet.

China is also cultivating its relationship with Myanmar, through which
it hopes to build a naval and military presence in close proximity to In-
dia--a long-time rival--and the Indian Ocean. This is a way for China to

reach that critical body of water without potential hindrance from other Southeast Asian countries. A growing Chinese presence in Myanmar is a sign of China's growing role and it presents a direct challenge to India and the rest of the region.[25]

Both history and current events prompt small Asian nations to eye China's assertiveness and Japan's economic power warily. Singapore probably speaks on behalf of many when it welcomes an American presence in the area to balance the two regional powers.[26]

For the future, the Pacific region will most likely see a balance of power between China and the United States, with a sensible Japan restricting itself to a civilian role. An alternative is an emergence of a common "Asian system."[27] Japan's situation as the dominant economic and political power at least in offshore Asia is unique because of its residual reluctance to exercise military pressure. Another anchor--and an obvious political ally of Japan's--of offshore Asia is Australia. In the 1990s, its orientation towards Asia-Pacific became more concrete in political and economic terms. As has been said by one prominent observer, "The question is not whether Australia is Asian but how it can best adjust to being Asian."[28] One can expect that Australia will try to play a mediating role in Asia-Pacific affairs in the near future. Later on, it may have reasons to actually ally more closely with the Asian countries. Much will depend on the behavior and orientation of Japan.

The extent and pace of development of that Asian constellation over the long run will be the key element in the international system of the 21st century. In the middle of the 1990s, however, the extremely diverse institutions and policies of the various industrializing countries in the area cannot really be called a common system, even without the dwarfing impact of the two giants and their respective--often antipathetic--tendencies. Thus, in the short run, scholars like Paul Krugman are partly correct.

India, with a population of almost 900 million and a rather steady economic growth of between 4% and 6%, is adjacent to China and the Pacific region. Its role remains open. If current reforms succeed, India will have a much more open and modern economic structure. India's economic reform process follows the classic Bretton Woods approach of identifying state restrictions on industry and hoping that growth will be spurred by progressively removing these constraints. Even when the Bretton Woods approach attempts to pay attention to agriculture, it emphasizes the costs industrial development programs impose on same, viewing their removal as supportive of agricultural development. As Manuel F. Montes notes, "China's approach did not follow this process. It did not start by removing restrictions on prices, but instead started with improving incentives and incomes for farmers."[29] India's long-term growth is now more predicated on international economic developments than it was in the 1980s; consequently, India needs global free trade. Yet its political situation remains unstable despite its democratic traditions, creating protectionist temptations.

India is politically weak--conflicts between national groups, religions and castes are a major structural problem. A weak India will remain isolated, a more assertive one risks running into conflict with China. India should perhaps aim for a regional role in South Asia compatible with China's design. India will certainly seek a more assertive regional role, in both South Asia and East Asia. Its dominance in a divided South Asia is not seriously threatened by the United States, Russia or even traditional nemesis China, and the loss of Soviet support did not change, as Saul B. Cohen states, "India's geopolitical sway over the region." In general terms, the power vacuum caused by the withdrawal of Soviet support from Southeast Asia (particularly in Vietnam and elsewhere in Indochina) has been filled increasingly by China and India.[30]

Mastery of the Heartland:
The Emergence of an "Orthodox" Russia

"The West has no strategy to deal with the threat of post-Soviet integration."
--Adrian Karatnycky

"Like the old Eastern Roman Empire, the Soviet Union (and Russia) is an uneasy amalgam of East and West. It is also one of the main territorial buffers between the populous, quarrelsome, and...militarily sophisticated states of the Middle East and Southern Asia and the wealthy Western democracies."
--Andrew C. Coldberg

"While Russia is a secular state and most Russians, like most Westerners, are secular in their outlook, Russia is also the core state of a major civilization historically identified with Orthodox Christianity."
--Samuel Huntington[31]

The collapse of the Soviet Union in August 1991 was one of the most important geopolitical events of the 20th century. The significance of this event has been compared to both the French and Russian revolutions and the two World Wars. As a consequence of this historic turning point, post-Soviet Russia was relegated to a secondary position in world politics.[32] It was no longer on par with the United States, except for strategic military capability. It should be emphasized, however, that the Russian-led Eurasian coalition of states will remain in a position to dominate its geostrategic realm--a vast spatial arena large enough to affect the areas within its strategic-military reach. Consequently, in defining realms as continental and maritime, the reference encompasses not only lands and climates but also outlooks. The Eurasian continental world, *Heartlandia*, is more isolated, more inwardly-oriented, and more heavily endowed with raw materials than its maritime counterpart.[33] The future position of Russia in the international system depends primarily on its evolution in two dimensions: stability and geographic focus.

Will reforms lead to a stable economic and political system? On this count, the economy will be the decisive factor--a stable political system cannot be built without a stable and advancing economy. Desperate people are bound to choose desperate alternatives, which abound in Russian domestic politics. In brief, the primary threat with which the "new" Russia and the independent republics associated with it must deal is "domestic"--civil discord and frustration, not external attack.

That said, Russian strategic planning must confront several tasks over a continuum of considerations that begin domestically but which easily cross national borders. First, Russia must ensure control over the panoply of nuclear weapons. This requires managing the military establishment, preventing internal differences within the officer corps and between it and enlisted soldiers, institutionalizing civilian authority over the armed forces, and preserving the command of the nuclear warheads in the former Soviet Union. Second, Russia must assure that no foreign actor can attack it. Third, Russia must cement the Commonwealth of Independent States (CIS) into an integrated confederation that can create also a military "defense space." In what is left of the CIS, Russia, as principal heir to the vast Soviet strategic arsenal, remains a militarily strong entity despite its retreat--which to some observers was involuntary--from external involvements. Russia remains the largest and most heavily armed state in Europe.[34] In this regard, in particular, China and the Muslim countries to the south, and perhaps Germany (read NATO), present potential, if unknown, threats.

Russia's aggregate production declined by 50% in the 1990s, and the country has been among the worst performers among transition economies. But there is another side to this as well. The economy did not collapse, basic social and economic functions continued to be maintained, there were no widespread social disturbances (for all its media-grabbing ferocity, the 1993 battle between President Boris Yeltsin and the parliament did not betoken intense alienation between Yeltsin's government and large segments of the population) and, though inequality undoubtedly widened, average consumption levels declined by much less than statistical production.[35] None of the frequently-discussed catastrophe scenarios came to fruition by the mid-1990s, and one should prepare for the eventuality that they will fail to materialize in the latter part of the decade as well. Moreover, due to its immense geographic size, nuclear weapons and natural resources, Russia will remain a superpower in the future, or at least a quasi-superpower. This should be the starting point for any of the analysis concerning the emerging new world system.

The Russian state--that is, the political organization of the society--has remained weak during the post-communist era. Traditionally, Russia has been characterized by a chasm between far-reaching state ambitions and available resources. In plain economic terms, in 1992-93 the Russian state was strong enough to collect taxes but too weak to control expenditure and implement legislation. Since late 1993, even the capacity to collect taxes has been in jeopardy. The weakness of the state is also obviously reflected in its capacity to use, project and signal power at home and abroad. This has been proved by the rather Pyrrhic campaigns in Chechnya. However, the catastrophic scenario of eventual dissolution of the Russian state remains of low probability, but with at least some plausibility.

Economic recession in Russia began in 1990 and it has not ceased, with output down by as much as 50%; in Eastern Europe, recession lasted on average for three or four years, reducing output 20%-30%. If the Russian economy started to grow in 1997 at an average 5% per annum rate, it would take 11 years (to 2007) to achieve pre-1989 levels of GDP. It may be tempting to characterize, as Sergei Popov does, the emerging Russian (and CIS) market structure as one that combines the features of both European and Asian models. The evolving Russian market economy is not, however, going to be compatible with the European or East Asian pattern. The closest analogue may be probably found in some of the Latin American archetypes of the 1970s--very high wealth and income inequalities, strong social tension and poor social consensus about reform, large unreformed latifundias in agriculture, non-competitive sectors in industry supported by government subsidies, economically and politically weak regimes whose commitments stretch beyond financial capacities, resulting in numerous cases of government failure, outbursts of inflation and capital flight, discouraged savings, investment and growth. To change the "Latin American" scenario into a more favorable one, noncosmetic reforms are required. As has been stressed, "the political feasibility of such a scenario does not seem to be high, though some moves in this direction are likely."[36]

The domestic problems and the old structures of the Russian economy may constitute an obstacle for Russia in joining international economic organizations. As a result, a protectionist Russian economic area may emerge. Jack F. Matlock, former US Ambassador to the Soviet Union, notes that "even economic liberals are calling for protectionist measures to revive industrial production."[37] In fact, a number of former Soviet states are preparing to join the WTO, but would almost certainly be unprepared to enter into an arrangement leading to global free trade.[38] The protectionist interests may link the former states of the Soviet Union (such as Belarus, Kazakhstan, Georgia and even Ukraine) closer to the Russian Federation in the longer term. This development would have geostrategic repercussions.

As Samuel Huntington reasons, "as the core state, Russia's primary responsibility is to maintain order and stability among Orthodox states and nations."[39] One can assume that this task will legitimize the existence of Russia as an empire also in the future.

The geographic focus, however, of an "Orthodox Russia" is not simply congruent with the reach of orthodox culture. Both Petrine and Soviet Russia had a European vocation, and in the early 1990s Russia was still --in geographic and political terms--basically a "European" state. Strategically, however, it has three faces, looking respectively westwards (to the rest of Europe and to the Atlantic), eastwards (to East Asia and the Pacific), and southwards (to the Near and the Middle East)--the last named probably the area of greatest threat to the country's security and stability.[40]

The threat of a military confrontation between Russia and the Euro-Atlantic community has not fully disappeared, however. With the disintegration of the Soviet Union, Russia has lost its direct access to Central Europe via Ukraine and Belarus. Indeed, Russia is becoming more isolated from the rest of Europe. Russia's oil production--and foreign currency revenue--is declining largely because of outdated technology and the loss of access to appropriate processing locations on its own territory (much of the Soviet-era energy exportation industry was located in the Caucasus). This may have both geopolitical and strategic repercussions in the 1990s.[41]

Among the new elite of Russian scholars and decision makers, there is debate about the country's new international profile and identity. Many emphasize Russia's need to focus on internal affairs during the forthcoming one or even two decades, which would give the country time to consolidate economically. Simultaneously, Russia should develop a new geopolitical strategy which better takes into account its new--diminished--international status. According to this strategy, Russia should have a balanced relationship with China, the United States and Europe--it should not, therefore, unequivocally align with any of these powers.[42]

In contrast, others point out that the major military threat to Russia is not located on the western reaches of its security zone (as it was when NATO was lined up opposite Soviet troops at the Fulda Gap in East Germany), but rather in the melange of Caucasian "Bosnias" and unstable or potentially unstable Muslim regimes on its own southern borders (i.e., Russia's frontiers, not those of a satellite state). This has lead to speculation about Russia having a different strategic perception than the Soviet Union. While the Soviets perceived the West as a threat, Orthodox Russia has to keep guard on its southern flank vis-a-vis an Islamic world. From Russia's point of view, this could mean that the West has changed from a threat to an anchor of stability and a respected--even sought-after--partner. A new post-Cold War reality is that the center of gravity of "Europe" (that is, Germany and the European Union) is shifting eastwards. For Russia, this is primarily a new challenge, not necessarily a threat.

The geopolitical consequences of Soviet disintegration, however, are perhaps too recent for a definitive conclusion. While most Russians seemed to accept the goal of keeping Chechnya a part of Russia in 1995, many political leaders of a "nationalist Russia" point out that the country "...has no sensible way out other than to recognize the independence of the Chechen Republic. All possible arguments speak in favor of this."[43]

This view expresses the realistic argument that in order to safeguard the existence of the core of a Slavic-Orthodox Russian empire, such "non-organic" parts as the Chechen Republic, which has an Islamic heritage and was never a willing constituent part of Russia, must be jettisoned. Areas having little cultural or ethnic affinity with the mother or core state do not logically fall within the purview of this constellation, and their involuntary membership within it will only weaken its viability.

Russian domestic stability depends on a delicate balance between economic reform and the ability to maintain the core of the organic Russian state unified. Outsiders can only have a limited influence on the fate of Russia's reforms, as--given the scope of the problems facing the country --foreign help is only "a drop in the ocean." This does not mean, however, that Western nations should leave Russia to its own fate. Moreover, grandiose political gestures and over-publicized aid packages may do more harm than good by allowing anti-reformists to depict reformers as western stooges. Instead, Russia should be given a nominal but honorable rank that suits its former status and prestige; additionally, its participation in common institutions should be courted. These measures can help consolidate Russian reforms and the country's fragile democracy, and thus have a profound impact on the international system to come.

From a geostrategic perspective, however, Russia's relationship with China will be the most crucial question in the long term. The "heartland" of Halford Mackinder is at stake. The Soviet Union assumed the role of the land power during the Cold War. However, it was in conflict with China, which shares the bulk of this "world island." With China's rise, Russia is likely to lose the mantle of the land power to its Asian neighbor, and it is possible that many Asian CIS republics will switch allegiance from Moscow to Beijing. Yet without Russia, China masters only a limited part of the heartland. The Soviet Union had access to both the Atlantic and the Pacific, and on many occasions attempted to secure access to the Indian Ocean. China has only access to the Pacific, although it is seeking a presence in the Indian Ocean via its relationship with Myanmar.

The geographic scope of China is more limited than that of the Soviet Union, although the Chinese seek to compensate through economic development, which will provide them with resources far greater than those that had been available to the Soviets. A rising China aligned with Russia will unite the heartland and challenge others on an unprecedented scale. Recent history, however, makes such a pairing difficult to foresee. Within 10 years of the communist triumph in the Chinese Civil War in 1949, Mao Zedong began to resent his erstwhile Soviet allies for what he believed was lack of due regard. In the early 1960s, the two communist giants grew apart diplomatically, and by the end of the decade the two countries actually clashed in a border dispute on the Amur River in Manchuria separating them.

While the border issue has been resolved, the two countries retain heavy military dispositions in the area. Such a wary mutual relationship works to Western advantage, for a close strategic partnership between Russia and China is not in the West's interest. The maritime power(s) should keep the heartland divided. This can be accomplished by giving Russia incentives to cooperate, for example by giving it access to western institutions.

Yet the question of the geographical focus of Russia's strategic perception remains as open as that of its internal stability, although by the middle of the 1990s a consolidation of its foreign policy in the "near abroad" (the former constituent republics of the Soviet Union) and some parts of Eastern Europe, such as Slovakia, was evident. In the years 1992-1993 the tide was still in favor of a loosening Commonwealth of Independent States, but by 1994-1995 this policy changed and Russia had begun strengthening its hold on CIS republics, primarily by economic means, because Russia keeps to a large extent the economic lifelines of other CIS states in its hands. Consequently, at least some of the members of the CIS, such as Belarus, have worked towards close relationships, which could even lead to a consolidation of some parts of old Soviet territory by the end of the decade.[44]

Russia's "new-found" assertiveness is also evident in Europe, where the Bosnian conflict has constituted a good laboratory of Russia's relationship with western powers. Russia was long critical of NATO's apparent bias against the Serbs in Bosnia. This has underlined the strategic problem of the Balkans, divided as the area has always been between eastern and western influences, interests and conflicts. Europe's place in the new international system depends much on Russia's choices and place in the world.

As "Orthodox Russia" seeks its geopolitical status in the 1990s, democratic and anti-democratic forces alike in the country are both trying to avoid isolation and further diplomatic decline, not necessarily for widely varying reasons. If Russia does not become a more organic part of Europe and the Euro-Atlantic security partnership, it may assume the role of geopolitical "wild card" between the rising China and Europe as well as within the Euro-Atlantic security structure itself. This scenario would have a most negative impact on world security in the early 21st century.

The Middle Eastern Riddle

"The Islamic resurgence will move forward, and governments throughout the Islamic world will be under continuous pressure to define their identity and their interests in Islamic terms. Islam has bloody borders. They are likely to remain bloody."

--Samuel Huntington[45]

It is obviously misleading to talk about either the Middle East or Europe as well-defined, discrete, homogenous entities. In our post-modern age, it is evident that, for instance, Sicily has more in common with Lebanon than with Estonia, Greece with Egypt than with Denmark, Spain with Morocco than with Poland. The Middle East is divided into a number of sub-regions (the Maghreb, the Valley of the Nile, the Mashriq, the Arabian Peninsula and the Gulf, and the non-Arab Middle East). What unites this area is the Islamic religion and its imperial history. Each of these subregions, however, has its own set of cultural identities, political idiosyncracies, and economic specificities, perceptions and concerns. It is difficult to get these regions to unify on any major questions after the apparent solution of the problem of Palestine through Israeli-PLO entente.[46]

The Middle East, crucial in international affairs because of its geographic location and energy reserves, will remain a major destabilizing factor in world politics. At the meeting point of Europe and Asia and as the chief supplier of crude oil to the industrialized world, its future is a question mark for the coming geopolitical world order. The area finds itself at a crossroads of three possible paths to the next century: a path of economic and social maturity, nationalistic renaissance, or Islamic fundamentalism.

A theory on the emergence of democracy points out that democracy--a pluralist control of political power--is bound to emerge when resources spread to such an extent that no one social group can control the economy.[47] According to empirical evidence, many Arab countries with growing middle classes are on the verge of democracy. Coupled with the Middle East peace process, the democratization of Arab politics may make the region a factor of stability in world politics.

The pacification of the Middle East is not, however, a straightforward or unproblematic process. Even if structural evidence points towards emerging democracy, the advent of a democratic Middle East may not be easy. It can be imagined that internal tension within rich feudal oil producers may even lead to popular but autocratic regimes and military take-overs where Nasser-type nationalist leaderships may use oil wealth for political means: Islamic consolidation, a pact between rich oil producers with small populations with population-rich non-producers, an exchange of wealth for Arab unity. This kind of Arab-nationalist international actor could also well challenge the trilateral order of western nations.[48]

Western commentators have long focused on the threat of Islamic extremism in the Middle East. Islamic fundamentalism is in essence a social reaction to the modernization of Arab societies, much as fascism was in Europe in the 1930s. But Islamic fundamentalism does not provide an answer to the current problems of Arab societies and--despite its appeal--it is likely to be overshadowed either by emerging stability through economic and political modernization or by Arab nationalistic order. The civil war in Algeria, a result of the rise of political Islam, may foreshadow the beginning of major military conflicts within Islamic reaches. It is not inconceivable that Western states will soon need a new strategy of "containment," one directed, not vis-a-vis Russia or China, but rather against Islamic fundamentalism.[49]

As in other regions of the world, the states and governments of the Middle East have not been able to ignore the pressures for economic and political liberalization. The four North African states, as well as Turkey, Jordan and Pakistan, are either in the midst of, or have just completed, structural adjustment programs backed by the IMF. Practically all of the other countries of the region, even the oil-rich Gulf states, have introduced market-based reforms to deal with their budget deficits and balance-of-payments difficulties. On the political front, the Middle East has not followed the same democratizing trend to be seen in Latin America, Russia, East Asia and sub-Saharan Africa, but there have nevertheless been significant moves towards greater political pluralism in countries such as Jordan, Yemen, Kuwait and Egypt. The advances made in the Arab-Israeli peace process, in particular on the Palestinian and Jordan tracks, provide additional evidence that the region is heading, at least for the time being, towards economic growth and regional political stability.[50]

However, ever since the collapse of the Ottoman Empire, the Middle East has been one of the most contradictory and conflict-ridden regions in the world. It is rarely the case in the Middle East that any one external power is capable of asserting its unchallenged dominance of the region. Normally, a number of competing powers struggle for influence, as with the European powers and the "Eastern Question" in the 19th century, France and Britain in the inter-war period, and the United States and the Soviet Union during the Cold War. As Roland Dannreuther puts it, "...wise analysts have not made themselves hostages to future predictions [concerning the region], as there are always figures like Saddam Hussein who can undermine the most carefully crafted scenarios."[51] However, the unilateral dominance of the United States in the 1990s is a consequence of two "victories"--the victory over the Soviet Union in the long struggle of the Cold War and the victory over Saddam Hussein's challenge to the international system in the Gulf War of 1990-91. As a consequence, the United States can for the first time pursue its policies in the region without encountering a countervailing and opposed force as powerful and obstructive as the Soviet Union.[52]

Russia has, however, gradually been consolidating its power in the Middle East. This is not surprising--from the Russian perspective, the Middle East is a region geographically close to its southern borders, where it inevitably has distinct security and strategic interests not necessarily shared by more distant powers, such as the United States. In particular, Russian has historically been--and will continue to be--interested in the countries of the "northern tier" (the Caucasus, Central Asia, Turkey, Iran and Afghanistan). Nevertheless, Russia will likely emphasize cooperation with the United States in the Arab-Israeli peace process and elsewhere where its interests are not immediately at stake.[53]

Since the end of the Cold War, Russia's most vital security interests are related to Eurasia in general and Central Asia in particular. This region could become subject to Russian hegemony under the umbrella of the CIS. This power position would make it easier for Russia to be a real player in the Middle East, too. There are a number of so-called "pivotal states" in the region--e.g., Egypt, Algeria, Turkey and Pakistan-- which may increasingly become targets in a new big power rivalry. Today, the United States and Russia have also to take into account the European Union, not necessarily as a natural ally for one or the other but rather as a regional power in the Middle East in its own right.[54]

In any analysis about the prospects of peace in the Middle East one has to focus on oil. The oil resources of the region will become increasingly a source of political rivalry between the emerging new power centers. The Asia-Pacific region alone, which in 1996 consumed around a quarter of the world's energy, could account for 40% of the increase in global energy demand over the next 15 years. As a result, Kent Calder states, "Asia cannot avoid deepening its dependence on the low-cost Middle East."[55] This development has political and military repercussions. The question is whether a specific "Islamic-Confucian" connection will emerge. Iran, Iraq and Pakistan have become the primary Middle Eastern recipients of Chinese arms sales. In order to strengthen its position in the oil markets of the region, China can also easily supply its nuclear technology (particularly to Iran and Iraq).[56] One can predict a destabilizing strategic alliance between a number of Islamic states and China in the early 21st century as a result of the fight for low-cost oil in the Middle East. If such an alliance materializes, the global system-- whatever form it takes--might remain stable, but it will be fragile and potentially dangerous.

The question is whether a new security order and a balance of power can be established in the Middle East at the end of the 1990s. As the only true superpower left, the US is determined to maintain the favorable global balance and to use its predominance of military power to shield its declining relative economic power. The strategy may collide with the European Union's, let alone Russia's and--increasingly--China's own plans, in the Middle East in particular. Partly the Gulf War, but more particularly the moral paralysis over the Bosnian tragedy bespeak the failure of the EU to forge a common and independent foreign policy and to make a principled stand on international crises. But even though observers such as Adel Safty believe "...the European Union, like the United Nations and Russia, has been neutralized, bypassed or completely ignored as a player in the emerging order in the Middle East...," the EU has put great emphasis on the strategic importance of the Mediterranean region, which by geographic implication makes the Middle East a critical area for it. The EU gives strong financial support to the modernization process in the Islamic world and tries to make it impossible for Arab states to pose a security threat to European interests in the future.[57]

I want to emphasize that the Middle East will remain or become one of the global power centers, not necessarily as a result of the process of the unification of Arab states around Islam, but rather as a result of the strategic importance of the region. At the very least, the Middle East is one of the real wild cards in the emerging geopolitical world. James Fairgrieve once referred to a "crush zone" of small buffer states between the sea powers and the Eurasian heartland. Crush zones and their borders remain fluid. One can use the concerpt of such a zone or "shatter-belt" in thinking of the Middle East. In the future, this situation may not change, as the area will be the subject of an increasing rivalry among the US, the EU, Russia and the Asian powers over oil, and because it remains so highly fragmented internally.[58]

The European Union:
A Big Germany or a Semi-Federal Superpower?

"This 'process of Europe' does not proceed without tensions and contradictions, and only future generations will detect its underlying logic."
--Bernd Hamm

"The prospect of a European Union which stretches from Sicily to the North Pole and from the Atlantic to the Black Sea means the familiar one-track route to integration has reached its limits."
--Werner Weidenfeld and Josef Janning

"A genuine European identity in the security and defense field is indispensible. It requires political will on the part of the Member States [of the European Union]."
--European Commission[59]

The collapse of communism created both hopes and agonies for Europe. In fact, as a result of the end of the post-Second World War bipolarity in 1989-1991, "Europe" was "redefined." No longer meaning the more prosperous western half of the continent, it has linguistically come to mean something far greater, both in terms of geographic locus and political significance. But even if it still connoted only the western part of the continent, the Europe of the 15-state European Union is one of the big powers, a subject and not an object of international relations.

Three scenarios are obvious for the future of this new/old entity: "Fragmented Europe"--a serious loss of commitment to the integration process in the West and a growing number of economic disputes among Union members and with Eastern Europe; "Fortress Europe"--an accelerated move in the face of perceived external threats towards a more inward-looking but tightly integrated Western Europe; and "Wider Europe"--the emergence of a clearer and more positive strategy than at present for integrating the economies of Western and Eastern Europe.

All these scenarios are taking place within the same European civilization. Compared with China or the United States, this civilization is still much more divided politically and economically. On the other hand, the European civilization extended across the globe during the 20th century. Yet "...despite European solidarity, the finally decisive rule was competition between [sic] the European nations. Thus in two world wars, the powers of Europe proper destroyed their hold on the rest of the world."[60] As a consequence, while the European *civilization* extended globally, European *political power* diminished dramatically after the Second World War. At the end of the 1990s, the question is whether the European Union as a principal actor of the European civilization is able to reach the status of a global power player or is doomed to remain an economic giant but a political dwarf.

The Maastricht Treaty created a new type of nonstate actor in world affairs in 1991. The founding fathers of "Europe" saw on the horizon a "United States of Europe" that would ameliorate the bitter antagonism, particularly between Germany and France, that had periodically plunged Europe into destructive wars. The EU remains, however, decisively a community of independent states which have pooled sovereignty in supranational organs for certain limited issue-areas; critical decisions are made by the Council of Ministers, where states dominate, and most decisions still depend on national governments for implementation.[61]

During 1996 and 1997, however, the EU is making another effort to strengthen its institutions and define its international identity: the Intergovernmental Conference. The aim of this IGC is to prepare the Union for enlargement and the establishment of a real political union among its member-states. The question remains though, whether the EU is becoming one of the big powers on the international scene or whether the EU's enlargement will cease this process definitively.[62] While national differences will remain, so will the possibilities for stronger consolidation. On the other hand, so will the possibilites for "disintegration and resurrection of intra-European discord or even war," as John Mearsheimer puts it.[63]

After a long period of significant work toward economic and political integration, the impulse within the West European community of states toward the "ever closer union" has to a considerable extent been put into question in the middle of the 1990s. The unification of Germany and the geopolitical changes which followed upset the old balances within the community of states and, at the same time, modified the driving force behind German commitment to further integration. A new "German Question" has arisen: If Germany translates its dominant position within the European Union into a similar role in Greater Europe, what will be the geopolitical and strategic repercussions?

The post-Cold War European Union is no longer entirely part of the strategic skeleton and geocultural skin of the American Cold War bloc. This is a paradox, because one could posit that, as a result of NATO's expansion toward Eastern Europe, the US role in a "Greater Europe" would be strengthened. During the Cold War, however, the European Community was a French-dominated entity, as France had come to replace Nazi Germany as the leading continental state--but with one crucial difference: The French needed cooperative instruments, not coercive ones, to maintain their dominance. It could be said that, from Paris' perspective, the EC's function was to keep the Russians and the Anglo-Saxons out, the Germans down, and the French on top. Consequently, France has worked to deepen the EC/EU, not widen it, a policy born of geopolitical--not economic--consideration. As Michael Lind states,

> Paris had (during the Cold War) its own geocultural myth to promote its geopolitical goals. The rival of the American myth of "the West" or "the Atlantic Community" was the myth of "Europe." The French-led "Europe" had a kind of anti-American substance. After the election of Jacques Chirac to the presidency of France, a new situation has emerged. As a result of the unification of Germany, France had to start promoting a policy which would better protect its interests within the changing international environment.[64]

The European Union is to a large extent the product of a historical cooperation between France and Germany. Paris has supported a federal Europe and has gained support in Bonn. As a result of German unification, however, the widening of the EU presents a puzzle for the French. "The expansion of the EU to the east, into traditional areas of German economic and cultural influence, would by itself doom the Gaullist vision of Europe as a car driven by France and pulled by Germany, as Lind puts the dilemma correctly.[65] Concerning the basic goal of the Maastricht vision, the question is, however, about the building of a semi-federal state structure containing both economic (European Monetary Union, for example) as well as political (European Political Union) elements. This arrangement should, then, constitute a binding system which would both dampen any individual national sentiment or tendency to gain hegemony and safeguard European economic competitiveness vis-a-vis the rest of the world.[66]

Whatever its intentions--and whatever the repercussions--Germany will find it increasingly difficult to drive "integrationist" policy in the 1990s. The bill for its own integration of the former communist German Democratic Republic is becoming too high. And even if its own commitment to both broadening and deepening the union (viz., increasing the EU's supranational powers and expanding its geographic writ) were unalloyed, Germany does not speak for the community. The less-than-stellar performance of the various Maastricht and accession referenda have prompted Germany to move away from a federalist position, although even this modified stance still leaves Germany in the ranks of Western Europe's most strident "Europeans." With the average unemployment rate remaining above 10% in the EU, its constituent peoples may become anti-integrationist and resist any new enlargement bills. It is not difficult to doubt that France, a country perhaps less ardent than Germany in regard to supranationality but of otherwise impeccable Eurocredentials, would be seriously prepared to sacrifice the interests of its agricultural sector (one of the prime beneficiaries of the distorted and distorting CAP) in order to facilitate the EU membership of Poland--an East European country heavily dependent on agriculture. However, the end of the enlargement of the European Union could have negative geopolitical repercussions in the long term.[67]

One of the most significant geopolitical phenomena of the past century has been the proliferation of nation-states within the international system. Many of these are either very small and economically weak or irredentist and separatist, unstable entities prone to terrorism for their political purposes. Another group of these new states can be described geopolitically as "gateway states" which are uniquely suited to promote world peace, in keeping with the more general rise of what Richard Rosencrance once called "trading states."[68] In this respect, the end of the Cold War caused another major geopolitical change--the emergence of a number of democratic states. In the 1990s, the trend remains the same--the proliferation of both national states and democratic states continues. This makes it possible to bring the democratic states into closer cooperation: The zone of peace enlarge accordingly. The development is most striking in Europe. As Saul Cohen reasons, "The most promising geopolitical mechanism for restoring the balance between the continental and maritime realms today is tied to the emergence of Central and Eastern Europe as a gateway region."[69]

The enlargement of the EU is still an open question in Europe. Although the process has started, it will continue to face a number of problems in the 1990s and beyond. However, rational arguments (such as strengthening security and promoting reforms in Eastern Europe) are obvious for the gradual enlargement of the union. Yet such rationality does not always mesh with political realities. Disputes on the establishment of the EMU, or the failure of the Intergovernmental Conference, could stop expansion process. Lykke Friis has concluded that failure to enlarge will have severe costs:

1. a major setback in Central and Eastern Europe's transformation will occur, which could force Germany to act as a unilateral "fire extinguisher," thus literally tearing the EU apart; and
2. the EU's credibility as a European organization defending democracy and human rights will be shredded.[70]

It seems obvious that Europe has to develop the EU as its anchor of stability and prosperity, and thus the Union's enlargement must be accomplished without major setbacks. Indeed, the IGC must consider such enlargement as critical an objective as it does the Union's institutional reforms.

Beyond the EU's enlargement, there must also be development of its international role and status. The Union should construct for itself a major role among other players on the world scene. EU presence and influence are needed in at least some of the major trouble spots around the globe. This was evident most recently in regard to Bosnia and the Dayton agreement. "As American influence and interest recede, they [the EU] would be welcomed."[71] This may be the real reason for Europe's growing influence on global affairs.

If integration is the key to a secure Europe in the immediate future, then it is obvious that the further enlargement of the union beyond 15 states will be a crucible. At the 1993 Copenhagen summit of the European Council, it was agreed to incorporate--gradually--the East and Central European states into the European Union; in 1994, at the Essen summit, the Council further agreed that the Baltic states would belong to this group as well. As a consequence, we know the emerging geographic size of the European Union. Will it be a federal union of 20-25 equal states in the future, or will there be different tiers of commitment, responsibility and benefit?

The goal of establishing a federal union, as reflected in the Maastricht Treaty, presupposed that renewed European integration would bring new economic growth and jobs. The inaccuracy of the assumed result has only exacerbated the theological debate throughout the continent about the quality of amalgamation, which was already inflamed because of visceral responses on issues of sovereignty and more empirical ones on issues of net benefit.

Consequently, the future of the European Union as an international actor depends much on its internal evolution. A deeper union may be a good thing in terms of international stability, as more effective decision making can better execute the responsibilities Europe will have to assume in keeping the world stable. In contrast, a union of nation-states is likely to be a union of *big* nation-states, giving an assertive Germany or ambitious France too many liberties from the point of view of their smaller European partners.

Enlargement, however, regardless of its quality, forces the European Union to face many of its still-unsolved internal questions. Most Europeans agree that the EU should absorb East European countries as new members, but the Union will have to make hard choices on how to adapt, how to make itself strong enough to be able to tackle these new challenges.

The biggest political question regards leadership, not of the Union, but rather of the continent. The unification of Germany, the country with Europe's biggest population and economy, extended a gradual process of de facto control of the EU. Consequently, without strong common institutions, the EU is bound to be only a big Germany, an echo of Germany's ambitions. This is why a more effective and closer union must evolve. Yet a "closer" union risks becoming an enlarged France, a protectionist-oriented Fortress Europe, with Paris deciding on its pace and direction. Incorporation, first of the European Free Trade Area countries, then of Eastern Europe, will prevent this from happening. Enlargement will probably force the EU to become a more coherent and mature entity.

The geopolitical role of the European Union is evolving. In particular, as a "German project," the EU has two basic concerns: It must be the vehicle for and the safeguard of the further unification of the whole of Europe, in particular the extension EU institutions towards Eastern Europe. Germany wants to avoid a situation whereby its eastern border is also permanently the EU's eastern border as well. At the same time, however, it must ensure that the region not turn itself into a Fortress Europe, but rather it must retain its extracontinental connections, particularly with the United States. Accordingly, German Foreign Minister Klaus Kinkel proposed the establishment of a Euro-Atlantic Free-Trade Agreement in Spring 1995.[72]

Closer cooperation on foreign and security policy is a prerequisite to the European Union that the visionary founders of the European Community once sought. The EU has acute security risks, primarily in the south, in the Mediterranean region, particularly in the Middle East and in Algeria. The threats in the Balkans are obvious but the Europeans can still work to contain them, albeit in a flawed manner; however, without any clear-cut strategies, they must do so in cooperative fashion with Russia, the US and the rest of the international community.

The relation that the EU will have with Russia is central to the future European order in the longer term. A peaceful and constructive relationship is much in the interest of all. I would argue that the EU should let military matters be channelled to the Atlantic partnership, rather than attempt--perhaps in vain--to forge an independent West European military entity. The Atlantic partnership keeps Russia balanced, while at the same time keeps a distinction between a civilian EU and military transatlantic organs. A civilian EU can best stabilize Eastern Europe, as its civilian nature constitutes less of a threat in Russia's perception.

Yet there remains a fundamental trap here. In 1995, it became obvious that Russia had great difficulties accepting any expansion eastward of NATO, which remains a key vehichle of Euro-Atlantic strategic partnership. A question even the "civilian" European Union must concern itself with is whether new security arrangements in Europe--the new "us"--will lead to a new political and military division on the continent, with Russia the new "them." How much emphasis should be given to the priority of maintaining a relationship of evolving partnership with Russia? If so, would it be better to develop an integrationist security policy for Europe around the European Union and its institutions, like the Western European Union? In this scenario, NATO would constitute a last resort for its current members, not a new security umbrella for the former Warsaw Pact countries.

Consequently, the EU should gradually develop its international role to cope with global challenges. This means that the EU should also have a more independent voice in hard-core security matters besides the Euro-Atlantic partnership through NATO. The Union should develop its role from a civilian power to a major political power which executes its military needs through IFOR-type arrangements.

Notes

1. Stuart Corbridge, "Maximizing Entropy? New Geopolitical Orders and the Internationalizing of Business," in George J. Demko and William B. Wood (eds.), *Reordering the World: Geopolitical Perspectives on the 21st Century* (Boulder, CO: Westview Press), 1994, p. 297; Kegley & Raymond, *A Multipolar Peace?*; Samuel Huntington, "The Clash of Civilizations," *Moscow News,* February 3-9, 1995; Edward Said, *The World, The Text, and the Critic* (London: Vintage), 1971, p. 171.

2. See Saul B. Cohen, "Geopolitics in the New World Era: A New Perspective on an Old Discipline," in Demko and Wood (eds.), *Reordering the World,* pp. 28-29.

3. Huntington, "Clash of Civilizations."

4. The problem of power and culture has been thoroughly discussed in Wilfried L. Amaturo, "Literature and International Relations: The Question of Culture in the Production of International Power," *Millenius,* Number 1, 1995, pp. 1-25. See also Michael Lind, "Pax Atlantica: The Case for Euramerica," *World Policy Journal,* Vol. 13, No. 1, 1996, pp. 1-7.

5. See Stephen Hobden, "Geopolitical Space or Civilization? The International System in the Work of Michael Mann," *International Relations,* Number 6, December 1995, pp. 77-102.

6. Joseph S. Nye, Jr., and Wiliam A. Owens, "America's Information Age," *Foreign Affairs,* March/April 1996, pp. 20-36. Nye defines "soft power" in his *Bound to Lead* as that which can rest on the appeal of one's ideas or the ability to set the agenda in ways that shape the preferences of others. This can also be described in terms of old-fashioned "ideological warfare" with liberal, not coercive, means.

7. See Luttwak, "From Geopolitics to Geoeconomics," pp. 17-24.

8. For a discussion of constructivism as one of the theoretical tools in analyzing post-Cold War international relations, see Chapter 7 in this book, which draws heavily from Wendt's key articles, "Anarchy is What States Make of It: The Social Construction of Power Politics," *International Relations,* Spring 1992, pp. 391-426, and "Collective Identity Formation and the International

States," *American Political Science Review*, June 1994, pp. 385-396.

9. Lind, "Pax Atlantica," p. 7; Liu Binyan, "Civilization Grafting: No Culture is an Island," *Foreign Affairs*, September/October 1993; Klare, "The Next Great Arms Race ."

10. Calder, *Asia's Deadly Triangle*; James Fallows, *Looking at the Sun: The Rise of the New East Asian Economic and Political System* (New York: Pantheon), 1994.

11. See Demko's and and Wood's *"Introduction: International Relations Through the Prism of Geography,"* in their *Reordering the World*, pp. 3-13. The authors use the concept of "geopolinomics" as a synonym for "geoeconomics"; the concept of "geoculture" refers to the combination of culture and geography as a structural factor of a state in the system.

12. See the preface to Calder's *Asia's Deadly Triangle*. See also Robert L. Paarlberg, "Rice Bowls and Dust Bowls," *Foreign Affairs*, May/June 1996, pp. 127-132.

13. Thurow, *Head to Head*; Paul Krugman, "The Myth of Asia's Miracle," *Foreign Affairs,* November/December 1994, and also George Hicks, "The Myth of the Asian Century," *The Wall Street Journal*, November 9, 1995. Hicks states that "the next century, like the last, will almost certainly be America's. Its technological lead in the production of both military and civilian goods is growing."

14. For the history of East Asia's economic growth, see Tommy T.B. Koh, *The United States and East Asia: Conflict and Cooperation* (Singapore: Institute of Policy Studies), 1995. Concerning Chinese economic growth, see Vaclav Smil's brief summary, "How Rich is China?" *Current History*, September 1993, pp. 265-269. See also *Communication from the Commission: A Long-Term Policy for China-Europe Relations,* (COM[95] 279 final; July, 1995). On the mercantilist cast of China's and Japan's trade policies, see Greg Mastel, "A New U.S. Trade Policy Toward China," *The Washington Quarterly,* Winter 1996, pp. 189-207.

15. For an interesting observation about the prospects for a trading bloc made up of Japan, Taiwan, Korea, Singapore and some other developing economies in southeastern Asia, see Thurow, *Head to Head,* pp. 84-85.

16. See Calder, *Asia's Deadly Triangle*, pp. 43-44, 99-100.

17. See, for example, Roh, *The United States and East Asia*, pp. 58-79, which contains a thorough analysis of the security of the Asian Pacific. See also Hugh DeSantis, "Europe and Asia Without America," *World Policy Journal*, Autumn 1993, pp. 33-43. Thomas L. Friedman stresses that Japan should not be underestimated, because it is capable of maintaining its power position through its companies, which are beginning to dominate the megamarket of tomorrow's Asia; see his "Japan: A Serious Country That Only a Fool Would Write Off," *International Herald Tribune,* March 4, 1996.

18. On China's increasing military spending, see Nicholas D. Kristof, "The Rise of China," *Foreign Affairs,* November/December 1993, pp. 59-74.

19. Kristof states that "the United States has possessed the world's largest economy for more than a century, but at present trajectories China may displace it in the first half of the next century and become the number one economy in the world." Kristof, "The Rise of China," p. 59.

20. For China's economic and political impact on the international system, see *Communication from the Commission.*

21. On China's internal economic and political problems, see, for example, Edward Friedman, "A Failed Chinese Modernity," *Daedalus,* Spring 1993, and "China's North-South Split and the Forces of Disintegration," *Current History,* September 1993, pp. 270-274.

22. See, e.g., Andrew J. Nathan, "Beijing Blues," *The New Republic*, January 23, 1995. According to one Chinese observer: " If we let our growth rate go below 6%, we cannot keep up with demand for jobs and will fall into social disorder due to unemployment."

23. Mastel, "A New US Trade Policy Toward China," p. 192.

24. Cohen, "Geopolitics in the New World Era," p. 26.

25. China's military tests near Taiwan in March 1996 demonstrated the return of power politics in East Asia. Some observers see in this phenomenon the rise of China's new nationalism as a product of a mixture of Maoism and Confucianism. See Steve Mufson, "China's New Nationalism: Mix of Mao and Confucius," *International Herald Tribune,* March 20, 1996.

26. In March 1996, the United States began to increase its naval presence in Asia as a result of China's military tests near Taiwan. Simultaneously, both Western and Asian officials insisted that only the United States was capable of keeping the strategically vital sea lanes open in the region. See Michael Richardson, "Asia Looks to U.S. to Protect Trade Routes Around Taiwan," *International Herald Tribune,* March 14, 1996. On the need to balance both Japan and China against each other, see Roh, *The United States and East Asia,* pp. 68-71.

27. Fallows, *Looking at the Sun.*

28. David Sanger, "Australia is Striving to be Asian, But How Asian?" *New York Times,* August 16, 1992.

29. Manuel F. Montes, *"Long-Term Projections for China and India,"* a paper prepared at Wider/UNU Institute, Helsinki, December 6, 1996.

30. With respect to India's growing economic and political role, see *The Economist,* January 8, 1994. See also Cohen's "Geopolitics in the New World Era," pp. 30-31.

31. Adrian Karatnycky, "Russia Isn't Supposed to Be Rebuilding a Soviet-Style Military Bloc," *International Herald Tribune,* August 31, 1994; Andrew C. Coldberg, "Challenges to Post-Cold War Balance of Power," in Charles. W.

Kegley and Eugene R. Wittkopf, (eds.), *The Future of American Foreign Policy* (New York: St. Martin's Press), 1992; Huntington, "The Clash of Civilizations."

32. For a discussion of Russian perceptions of their role in world politics, see Hannes Adomeit, "Russia as a 'Great Power' in World Affairs: Images and Reality," *International Affairs*, vol. 71, no.1, 1995, pp. 35-68.

33. Cohen, "Geopolitics in the New World Era," pp. 28-29.

34. See "Russia's Riddle of the Regions," *The Economist*, March 23, 1996. Concerning Russia's political development in 1995, see Alexander Yanov, "Gennady Zyuganov's Patriotic Communism," *Moscow News*, March 14-20, 1996.

35. Concerning the development of the world economy, see "International Business Statistics," *Statistics of Finland*, March 1996. For specific information concerning Russia's economy in the 1990s, see, e.g., Jagdish Bhagwati, "Shock Treatments," *The New Republic*, March 28, 1994.

36. Vladimir Popov, *"Is Russia Likely to 'Saddle' Economic Growth?"* a paper prepared for the Wider/UNU Institute, Helsinki, December 1996. Also, see the annex about possible Russian economic growth between 1995 and 2010.

37. Jack F. Matlock, Jr., "The Struggle for the Kremlin," *New York Review of Books*, August 8, 1996.

38. Charles R. Carlisle, "Is the World Ready for Free Trade?" *Foreign Affairs*, Voume 75, Number 6.

39. Huntington, "The Clash of Civilizations."

40. See Michael Mandelbaum (ed.), *Postcommunism: Four Perspectives* (New York: Council on Foreign Relations Press), 1996.

41. Russia's strong objection to the enlargement of NATO is an indication of this fear of isolation. Meanwhile, the western countries are not unified on the issue, which has become the source of a new potential geopolitical division in Europe. See Anatol Lieven, A New Iron Curtain," *The Atlantic Monthly*, January 1996, pp. 20-25. In 1996, the East Central European post-communist states started fearing a "new Munich" as a result of the delays in the enlargement process. See "Havel's Reminder to the West," *The Economist*, March 30, 1996.

42. See Adomeit, "Russia as a 'Great Power' in World Affairs."

43. For example, presidential candidate and former Soviet military hero Alexander Lebed, who later threw in with President Yeltsin, publicly opposed the Russian military interventions in Tajikistan and Chechnya, although his views began to "muddy" during the peace process he was commissioned to undertake. See Lieven, "A New Iron Curtain."

44. In the years 1994 and 1995, Russia's internal development contained a return of nationalism and an Orthodox-Slavic chauvinism, as demonstrated by the December 1995 elections for the Russian Duma. Gennady Zyuganov's "patriotic" communism gained strong support among the population. It is obvious that some of the post-Soviet Slavic states besides Russia--Kazakhstan, Belarus, and

Kirgizstan--are willing to consider the establishment of a Russian-led Slavic union, first economically and, later, politically, modeled on the European Union. Ukraine has tried to avoid this "remuscovization" process, but it has to balance between the Slavic gravitational pull and western integration. From a geopolitical point of view, the fate of this emerging Slavic entity is of crucial importance. However, a big shift of power within Russia itself in favor of some of the country's regions over the past few years may help the democratic forces hold on to their political leadership at the center.

45. Huntington, "The Clash of Civilizations."

46. With respect to the strategic situation in the Middle East after the Gulf War, see for example Adel Safty, "The Arab-Israeli Balance of Power After the Storm," *International Relations,* December 1994, pp. 51-74.

47. It is one of the key arguments of this book that promoting democracy and market economy is the wisest and least expensive investment that the western countries can make in their security. As President Clinton declared in a speech before the United Nations in September 1993: "Our overriding purpose must be to expand and strengthen the world's community of market-based democracies." About this argument in general, see Kegley and Wittkopf, *American Foreign Policy,* pp. 72-75.

48. On the failure of Arab nationalism and pan-Islam during the post-Cold War era, see Roland Dannreuther, *The Middle East in Transition* (Oslo: Institut for Forsvarsstudier), 1995, pp. 20-23.

49. Many countries in the Middle East besides Algeria face some kind of potential threat from growing Islamist opposition, most notably Egypt, Saudi Arabia and the emerging Palestinian entity. See Anthony Lewis, "Are Palestinians Really Committed to Peace?" *International Herald Tribune,* March 5, 1996.

50. See Michael C. Hudson, "After the Gulf War: Prospects for Democratization in the Arab World", *Middle East Journal,* No. 3, 1991, and August Richard Norton, "The Future of Civil Society in the Middle East," *Middle East Journal,* No. 2, 1993.

51. Dannreuther, *The Middle East in Transition,* p. 7.

52. Concerning this military and economic dominance of the United States in the Middle East, see, for example, Peter R. Odell, "International Oil: A Return to U.S. Hegemony," *World Today,* November 1994.

53. See, e.g., Roland Dannreuther, "Russia, Central Asia and the Persian Gulf," *Survival,* No. 4, 1993.

54. On Russia's policy in Central Asia, see S. Frederick Starr, "Making Eurasia Stable," *Foreign Affairs,* January/February 1996, pp. 80-92. The idea of a pivotal state--a hot spot that could not only determine the fate of its region but also affect international stability--has a distinguished pedigree reaching back to Halford Mackinder in the 1900s and even earlier; see Robert S. Chase, Emily B. Hill, and Paul Kennedy, "Pivotal States and US Strategy," *Foreign Affairs,*

January/February 1996, pp. 33-51.

55. Calder, *Asia's Deadly Triangle*, p. 59.

56. Alexander T. Lennon, "Trading Guns, Not Butter," *China Business Review*, March 1994. Also, Calder, *Asia's Deadly Triangle*, p. 123.

57. Adel Safty, "The Arab-Israeli Balance of Power," pp. 51-74. Concerning EU-Mediterranean cooperation, see, e.g., the *Barcelona Declaration* adopted at the Euro-Mediterranean conference in November 1995.

58. James Fairgrieve, *Geography and World Power* (London: University of London Press), 1915; in addition, see Cohen, "Geopolitics in the New Era," p. 32.

59. Bernd Hamm, "Europe: A Challenge to the Social Sciences," in Ali Kazancigill (ed.), *Europe in the Making* (Southampton: Blackwell Publishers/UNESCO), 1992, p. 3; Werner Weidenfeld and Josef Janning, "The New Europe: Strategies for Differential Integration," paper presented at the International Bertelsmann Forum, January 19-20, 1996, p. 7; *Reinforcing Political Union and Preparing for Enlargement*, European Commission Opinion on Intergovernmental Conference 1996 (manuscript completed in February 1996).

60. Hans-Heinrich Nolte, *"Europe in Global Society to the Twentieth Century,"* in *Europe in the Making*, pp. 23-39. Nolte states that "the globalization of the European system from the eleventh century onwards led in the twentieth century to preconditions for emancipation processes from European preponderance in the global society but not yet to a fundamental change in the rules."

61. On the history of European integration, see for example Robert O. Keohane and Stanley Hoffman, *"Institutional Change in Europe in the 1980s,"* in the book they edited, *The New European Community: Decision Making and Institutional Change* (Boulder: Westview Press), 1991, pp. 1-39.

62. For a brief analysis about the needs to develop a politically and strategically strong European Union, see Weidenfeld and Janning, "The New Europe"; see also the European Commission's *Reinforcing Political Union*.

63. Mearsheimer, "Back to the Future," p. 5.

64. Lind, "Pax Atlantica."

65. Ibid.

66. For the history and future prospects of the EU, see, for example, Michael O'Neill, *The Politics of European Integration: A Reader* (London and New York: Routledge), 1996.

67. About the European Union as an economic actor in the world economy, see Kegley and Wittkopf, *World Politics*, pp. 170-172.

68. Rosencrance, *The Rise of the Trading State*.

69. Cohen, "Geopolitics in the New World Era," p. 38.

70. Lykke Friis, A Look into the Crystal Ball: Scenarios for Eastern Enlargement, prepared for the International Political Science Association seminar on "The European Parliament, the Commission, and the Intergovernmental Confer-

ence of 1996," Brussels, July 3-5, 1996.

71. Francis Deron, Phillipe Pons and Jean-Claude Pomonti, "An EU Voice in the East Asia Security Debate," *International Herald Tribune,* July 22, 1996.

72. In *The New Europe*, Weidenfeld and Janning propose that a system of European-American Political Cooperation (EAPC) should be established along the lines of European Political Cooperation. The EU and the US need this primarily to contribute to the establishment of a transatlantic free trade zone.

5

Toward a New Global Rivalry

"Change is endemic to world politics, but one constant stands out: great-power rivalry for position in the hierarchy of nations."
                    --Charles W. Kegley, Jr. and Eugene R. Wittkopf

"Even Asian governments critical of China's authoritarianism and human rights record, or fearful of its ambitions, see their future economic performance bound up with that of China and its 1.2 billion consumers."
                    --Sandra Sugawara

"The military threat that brought China, Japan, and the United States into a strategic alignment against Moscow ended with the breakup of the Soviet Union. Now, East Asian stability depends on a more fickle and delicate relationship among Beijing, Tokyo and Washington."
                    --Michael Richardson

"Great powers are like divas; they enter and exit the stage with great tumult."
                    --Fareed Zakaria[1]

The Global Geopolitical Transition

This volume tries only to cope with the most important trends in world politics and, then, to elaborate on the emerging power centers and their relations as well as on their overall impact on international security. I have tried to look at world politics primarily as a system with patterns of interaction among constituent parts (power centers). I have had a macroscopic perspective and tried to discuss general trends and patterns of behavior instead of particular events.

In the two previous chapters, I have tried to formulate the evolution of the post-Cold War geopolitical order and its changing foundations. In this chapter, I will deal with the ongoing transitional period, which I call the "complex system," as a process toward new rivalry, and particularly with its next step. In sum, since the end of the Cold War, the development and transition of the global geopolitical system can be characterized as follows:

1. During the period of "unipolar momentum," which lasted from the fall of the Berlin Wall (1989) to the end phase of the Gulf War (1991), the international system was dominated by the United States, the only truly credible superpower. The system was basically stable, a result of the "accepted hegemony" of the US. The United Nations enjoyed a strong reputation during this time.

2. The emergence of the complex transitory system of the "post-unilateral momentum period," which began in 1992. This system has experienced the emergence of a multipolar order, which consists principally of the most powerful nations as key players: the US, Japan, Germany (the European Union), Russia and China. This transitional phase will last until the early years of the next century (perhaps until 2010), and it will be less stable than its predecessor largely as a result of the lack of dominance by any one player. This transitory system should experience a fundamental change in its foundations, as the most economically dynamic states will also gain increasing political influence (this is most apparent in the case of China).

3. This complex system will evolve into a new global geopolitical order based to a large extent on trading blocs, rather than on nations as such. These "political trading blocs" may be able to create a positive interrelationship among themselves, but a feasible alternative is an increasingly conflictual rivalry. If the latter, then a "cyclical hegemonic war" could take place some time in 2020-2025 when a major shift in global power relations occurs as a result of China's consolidation of its position.

My own assumption--and one of the key arguments of this volume--is that such conflictual rivalry is, in fact, likely. Even if only one of the key actors challenges the system's hierarchy, problems over the hege-monic "pecking order" may result.[2]

Cycles of war and peace have dominated 20th century world politics. The dramatic change has created both "new geopolitics" as well as a new geopolitical order as the foundations of power have shifted from military factors to economic ones. However, one can doubt that great power ri-valry as such would have faded away. On the contrary, although the im-mediate threat of great-power war seems to be over, great-power rivalry remains. The post-Cold War peace is fragile and dangerous.

The essence of "new geopolitics" derives more from the future than the past. Not only geography and military might, but also economic ef-ficiency and cultural creativity condition the geopolitical codes of emerg-ing great powers.

The old geopolitics certainly simplified the world map, which could be divided into two without the necessity of considering the underlying and sometimes changing subdivisions themselves. Consequently, American Cold War geopolitical practice produced the doctrine of rigid contain-ment and the theory of the falling dominoes, as well as other diplomatic constructions. As Saul B. Cohen states,

...it also influenced US leaders to reject any strategy that would accomo-date overlapping spheres of influence (as in the Middle East) or the desires of some states to remain uninvolved (e.g., India, which upon achieving its independence sought to maintain its neutrality).[3]

One can say that the end of the Cold War presents an opportunity to promote an understanding of the dynamic and holistic, almost organic, nature of geopolitical and geoeconomic processes.

In contrast to the old geopolitics, which was basically an instrument of military might, the new geopolitics can be applied to the advance of in-ternational cooperation and peace. The new geopolitics focuses primar-ily on the evolution of the political world as an interdependent system at varying scales, that is, from the national and transnational to the subre-gional and local. According to the old geopolitical view, the southern continents (Subsaharan Africa, South America) are fast becoming "quar-terspheres of strategic marginality" because the need for forward military bases has been so dramatically reduced. The representatives of the new geopolitical thinking, however, insist that precisely because a politically and economically unstable quartersphere is a cause of potential global instability, it warrants strategic attention even though the Cold War need for military bases has passed.[4]

I partly dispute both the old and the new geopolitical thinking, although both schools contain important elements. Every international system is under constant change--even the Cold War balance was based on dynamic equilibrium. Otherwise, no peaceful change could have taken place in the late 1980s. In this volume, I have tried to design new geostrategic realms or spheres of influence of the emerging political trading blocs. This system is in constant flux. It contains both processes of the dissolution of nations and empires as well as those of the unification of regions and states.[5]

The military equilibrium of the Cold War, however, has been superseded by an overarching set of "equilibristic" forces (e.g., capital flows, technology transfer, multinational corporations, communications networks, etc.) which are usually global but which certainly have regional origins. One can ask why no collapse or global confrontation has taken place in the face of these processes, which do contain threats to the integrity of the nation-state, even though on their faces they also strengthen the conditions of peace.[6]

I have listed three basic assumptions why the international system remains unstable despite--or perhaps because of--the broadening of these pacifying global forces:

1. *Protectionist pressures are growing in different parts of the world.* With the world's open trading system under serious threat--despite the conclusion of the Uruguay Round--international institutions should redouble their efforts to reinvigorate and nurture a continuation of the cooperative habit of past decades.
2. *Cultural differences of the emerging trading blocs are too fundamental for the establishment of a global value space as a condition of lasting peace.* That is, a passive reliance on ostensibly shared mores and norms will not suffice to ensure security; an active search for peace-ensuring regimes based on clear appraisal and balance of national (or regional) interest must be encouraged and supported.

3. The growth of the Asian economies will lead to an increasing drive for strategic resources (e.g., oil, food and water) which may cause a conflictual rivalry between a number of the political trading blocs. In the final analysis, this will be the most important factor in the restructuring of the geopolitical map of the world in the early 21st century.

Consequently, there is no multilateral institution which has the capacity to maintain peace in the world system, although the United Nations has certainly been presented with opportunities galore since the end of the Cold War. As a result, the threat of major military confrontation and escalation remains. Institutions simply cannot guarantee peace and stability, which ultimately derive instead from democracy and prosperity at the domestic level. There is thus no global economic and democratic space in sight.

Moreover, the rivalry between the most influential powers will contain military aspects in the longer term. Consequently, the return of the "old geopolitics" may take place and the division of the world system into two rivaling "geopolitical systems" may result. Twenty years onward from the mid-1990s, we may experience a transitional period where no real hegemony exists but a hardening rivalry among the emerging trade blocs will take place.

Protectionist Pressures Under Globalization of Economy

"What's going on as protectionism is gaining ground? Answer: A break-down of one of the greater intellectual myths of this century--the idea that laissez-faire and free trade policies would allow economies automatically to adjust to each other and promote maximum economic progress for all."
--Gregory Clark[7]

The boundaries of the world's geostrategic realms and regions remain in a constant state of flux, and, as I have indicated in previous chapters, will be so for at least two more decades. Regions change their political and economic orientations (witness Eastern Europe), and nations switch their alliances. One of the most influential factors in this process is the globalization of the world's economies.

During the heyday of the Cold War, the two superpowers believed that they could influence all parts of their respective geostrategic arenas. This was not entirely possible, however, and two differentiated economic and political systems emerged, which had relatively little mutual interaction. First, the "western political bloc" changed as a result of the rise of Japan and the European Community as differentiated economic competitors vis-a-vis the US. Within the Eurasian realm, at roughly the same time, China challenged the Soviet Union, and later on the other members of the "eastern bloc" did the same. In time, these new power players, if not yet power centers, began to develop independent relations with other regions and states.

In the post-Cold War realm, the process toward unified economic regions has accelerated. A new complex and open world system has emerged, with "...overlapping spheres of influence, varying degrees of hegemony and hierarchy, national components and transnational influences, interdependencies, and pockets of self-containment."[8] However, the system change has basically been founded on the globalizing trends of the world economy.

Regional and global liberalizing initiatives have been mutually reinforcing since the European Common Market was created in the late 1950s. In the mid-1990s, economic regionalism had not derailed economic globalism. In real terms, about 60% of world trade took place within free trade agreements or among countries that had decided to achieve free trade by the middle part of the century's last decade. The EU had completed the "single internal market" and by 1995 had agreed with 12 Mediterranean countries (Euromed) to establish free trade by 2010. The 18 countries of APEC--including the US, Japan and China-- have committed themselves to "free trade and investment in the region" by 2010 for the higher-income members (who account for 85% of their mutual trade) and by 2020 for the rest. The 34 democracies of the western hemisphere will devise a Free Trade Area by 2005, building on the existing NAFTA structure. A number of smaller arrangements, including the ASEAN Free Trade Area (AFTA) and Mercosur (Argentina, Brazil, Paraguay and Uruguay) in Latin America, augment these totals.[9]

However, there were trends toward strengthening regionalism at the expense of globalism. The major regional arrangements, particularly NAFTA and APEC, were created in part by missed deadlines at the

GATT Uruguay Round, and were intended to serve as alternatives to the global regime, if necessary. As I have tried to argue in this volume, this process, if not controlled, most probably will result in political trading blocs. Moreover, the ostensible success of Uruguay may have only postponed such an evolution. As noted American scholar C. Fred Bergsten puts it,

> By joining East Asia and North America, APEC has eliminated any possibility of the three-bloc world that was so widely feared a few years ago, but a two-bloc world that would convey substantial dangers could still be created instead if APEC and Europe fail to work out satisfactory accommodation.[10]

The root cause of economic integration has been political by nature, that is, the eradication of military conflict from both Europe and the Pacific Rim. The political argument for integration has not disappeared, although economic integration has had its regional bias from the beginning. Furthermore, it is considerably less complicated to work out mutually agreeable arrangements with a few neighbors than with the full membership of the 120+ strong WTO.

Consequently, as the urgency of competitive liberalization has accelerated, the regional approach has increasingly come to the fore. The EU, for example, is focusing on its internal and regional (i.e., the IGC and eastward expansion), while Asian giants Japan and China pose continued threats to openness of the trading system; finally the United States is provoking tension, in particular with its European allies, when penalizing foreign companies for doing business with countries considered U.S. enemies.[11]

The pressure towards protectionism has domestic and political roots that cannot be fully controlled. Unemployment considerations in Europe and a general temptation to an "America First" mentality in the US have, at least temporarily, raised concerns in both Asia and Latin America, where fast-growing economies would greatly benefit from the opening of the markets in the US and Europe that increasingly seem ripe ground for protectionism.

Charles E. Carlisle notes that

free trade worldwide is a distant goal, fraught with difficulties, but regional trading arrangements have been somewhat easier to attain....[consequently many observers fear that] they could go too far and that the world could break up into hostile trading blocs.[12]

The trend toward regionalism in world trade is a fact, although not, as yet, a clear-cut one.

The results of the WTO report comparing trade with regions before and after the completion of regional trade arrangements does not support the conclusion that world trade is increasingly regionalized. The report's statistics show that intraregional trade declined somewhat between the late 1920s and the years immediately following World War II, then rose dramatically until the early 1970s, but grew only a miniscule amount between the latter date and 1993 in Western Europe, while actually declining slightly in North America. Only in Asia did intraregional trade grow significantly in those years. This latter development can be explained not by a nonexistent regional trade arrangement but rather by a large shift of direct investment, much of it Japanese, into manufacturing facilities in Asia. One can say this is regionalism, but it is of the healthiest kind, driven by commercial considerations.[13]

It is obvious that global free trade by 2010 would enhance the prosperity of all countries by underwriting the ultimate success of competitive liberalization. "It would preclude the risk that regional arrangements could develop into hostile blocs."[14] The question is who will take the leadership necessary to develop the global free trade regime that seems necessary for the 21st century? The WTO is not a fitting and dynamic instrument for such an exercise. I would like to propose that the preliminary work be done in a new forum, a kind of G-7 model applied to global trade liberalization. I am of the opinion that the existing "regional - trading blocs" described elsewhere in this volume could be the main actors in such a process. If the world is solely given over to the WTO, time may run short and the trading blocs may turn more hostile vis-a-vis each other. I fear that this will be the case.

The Emergence of an Asian Power Game

"Ultimately, Asia's dangerous new power game...threatens to destabilize Ja-

pan's traditional low-posture military orientation. It also threatens to provoke, over the long term, a serious arms race, centering on Japan and China,
that could have global implications."

--Kent E. Calder

"The Pacific Basin myth is similar to the Western or Atlantic Community
myth; its rival, a pan-Asian but not pan-Pacific ideology that would exclude
the United States, is the Asian equivalent of a Gaullist pan-European anti-At-
lanticism."

--Michael Lind[15]

During the 20th century, the great power rivalry has geopolitically focused on Europe and Russia, as well as on East Asia and the Western
Pacific. It makes sense, as John Lewis Gaddis reasons, "to view World
Wars I and II as a single European civil war, in which the nations that
had dominated world politics for the preceding five centuries managed
to transform themselves, through their fratricidal behavior, into second-
class powers."[16] Consequently, geopolitical influence shifted from Europe to its peripheries, with the United States and the Soviet Union as
joint beneficiaries during the Cold War decades.

After the end of the Cold War, another major geopolitical shift is taking place, and a global multipolar geopolitical order is emerging: *Europe* is attempting a comeback as a result of the emergence of the German-driven European Union; *Russia* is obliged to withdraw to its historical role as a primarily Eurasian, not global, player; the *United States*
tries to establish its role as a global partner through NATO, NAFTA and
APEC, as well as other possible arrangements; *Japan* has yet to find its
role as a political player among other great powers; and *China* is emerging as the real challenger of the multipolar stability.

Michael Mandelbaum has pointed out that the Strategic Quadrangle--
that part of the globe encompassing East Asia and the western Pacific
where the political and economic interests as well as the military forces
of the United States, Russia, the People's Republic of China and Japan
all intersect--has been, with Europe, one of the two centers of international politics in this century. As in Europe, great powers have confront-
ed one another directly there. And like Europe, it has been the site of
the world's most productive economies.[17] In the emerging multipolar

system, the East Asian quadrangle seems set to become the real focus of international politics in the early 21st century. However, although the European quadrangle will be less dangerous, a conflictual relationship between the Euro-Atlantic community of states and Russia will not fade away entirely.

The East Asian economies are increasingly becoming an engine of global development. The argument of this book is that this fact alone brings the focus of world politics to the East Asian strategic quadrangle. World peace will be at stake there more than anywhere else in the emerging multipolar system. The question, as Richard H. Solomon puts it, is which of the major powers will shape the emerging structure of the "burgeoning region."[18] In the forthcoming East Asian power game, the European Union and, I assume, to a large extent Russia will play only secondary roles, primarily as partners of one of the bigger players, in this case, the United States and China.

China's growing military and economic power is, of course, the main source of concern for Asia's future. It makes a continuing U.S. regional presence indispensable. One of the preconditions to secure that presence is that Japan should open its markets and promote trade liberalization. As Singapore's Senior Minister, Lee Kuan Yew, said in May 1995:

> If peace and stability, which Americans have helped to maintain over last 50 years, lead to an increasingly prosperous Japan, Korea, Taiwan...China, ASEAN (and) Vietnam, but an increasingly less prosperous U.S., I don't see the U.S. Congress voting funds for the renewal of the Seventh Fleet and all the other things necessary to maintain the balance.[19]

However, a trade war between Japan and the United States seems to be a continuing factor as a result at least partly of Japan's domestic difficulties in coping with new strategic challenges. Japan is not used to combining its economic power with diplomatic skills. It seems to fail in taking in particular political leadership in the region. Yet this leadership should be necessary in order to balance in harmony with the United States vis-a-vis the growing power of China.[20] In the middle of the 1990s, it became clear that China's creeping expansionism in the South China Sea could threaten open confrontation in the region, jolting the stability that has kept East Asia's economic miracle going.

Changing energy demand will restructure strategic relations globally at the end of the 20th century. This change results from the growth of the Asian economies. Asia accounts for about a quarter of world oil demand, but only 10% of supply. Future growth in Asia's oil demand will far exceed the increase in supply in the region. In the short run, East Asia's growing reliance on imported oil may change its relationship with the Middle East and with Russia. Before 1992, Chinese oil imports primarily came from Asia-Pacific nations, with Indonesia, Malaysia, and Australia accounting for more than half. But in 1993, the volume of Middle East imports exceeded the flow from Asia for the first time. Chinese oil imports are projected to reach two million barrels a day, or 100 million tons per year, by 2010. As John P. Ferriter of the International Energy Agency puts it:

China is destined to become a major force in the global oil market. As a result, there may also be a geopolitical shift with far-reaching strategic implications on traditional relationships between China, the Middle East and the former Soviet Union, but also with other Asian economies, and...Japan and Western industrialized nations.[21]

The heart of Asian, and in particular East Asian, security remains China. The other countries have only two alternatives--either to start containing or engaging the growing "Greater China." Energy aid is urgent to China. This is not possible without the strengthening of multilateralism in Asia. Here APEC plays a crucial role. The prospect of creating a free-trade zone in the Pacific by 2010 or 2020 can be a useful inspiration to liberal trade forces. It would also encourage internationalists within China. It is obvious that only by means of strengthening global and regional economic integration that the emergence of the Asian power game can be avoided. As Kent Calder reasons:

The most urgent problem is the need to integrate economic changes into a conventional security calculus: to understand, for example, how economic growth or changing energy demand generates new patterns of military competition, or domestic political instability that can have security consequences.[22]

The "loser" of the Asian power game seemed to be Russia. That

country, however, has been seeking a new great power status for itself
since the Summer 1996 re-election of President Boris Yeltsin. Since the
collapse of the Soviet Union, Russia has been gradually increasing its
Asian orientation. This may be a case of virtuous necessity, as Russia
has already lost its main Black Sea, Baltic and Caspian ports and has in
fact been "pushed" into Asia. As Mikhail Titarenko puts it,

> the Asia-Pacific area provides Russia with a realistic opportunity to be-
> come integrated into the global economy by taking part in all kinds of mul-
> tilateral economic projects....[Consequently], as distinct from Western Eu-
> rope, the Asia-Pacific region is waiting for Russia.[23]

There seems to be a growing interest in both China and Japan to
strengthen Russia's Asian vocation. If this trend continues, it could restructure the strategic balance of power in the region. As Michael Lind
states, "if the United States were to attempt to contain China, Japan
would more likely try to act as interlocur, to play the United States and
China against one another, than as a loyal ally."[24] If Russia's emerging
"Asian role" is added, the US could become the real loser in the region
in the early 21st century.

The Asian power game could restructure global power relations as we
know them. Although the role of the European Union would remain
marginal in Asia, the further strengthening of the system of political
trading blocs could force dramatic changes if the EU began to pursue
economic and strategic interests that are more "European" than "Euroat-
lantic." The ultimate nightmare: "...a Sino-European entente, uniting the
world's largest common market with the world's most populous great
power."[25]

Consequently, as argued in this book, the Washington-Beijing connection will become the key strategic factor in East Asia. In practical
terms, President Clinton has effectively downplayed the American view
concerning human rights violations in China. At the same time, though,
his administration has promoted the idea of a region-wide security dialogue by backing the formation of an Asian Regional Forum (ARF) in
association with the early ASEAN post-ministerial meetings. However,
as Richard H. Salomon argues, "collective security has never worked in
modern East Asia."[26] These actions were taken in favor of a less con-

frontational approach, and neither the diplomatic or academic communities should spare effort in trying to devise common direction for Sino-American security cooperation in the late 1990s.

In the final analysis, the most promising future for the coming period in East Asia is that of a combination of a loose balance of power embodying areas of political and economic cooperation among the states concerned, with the U.S.-Japan alliance as the stabilizing core of the region. It could sustain the movement toward ever more open markets in a way that will forestall the formation of an exclusivist East Asian yen-dominated trading bloc and will advance a Pacific Basin-wide economic and political community. The question which will then remain is whether the U.S.-led coalition of East Asian states and Japan--if realized--with its policy of appeasement which is reflected in Clinton's policy shift vis-a-vis China will find itself on the road toward a new "Munich"--a peace settlement which then would lead, not toward a lasting "peace in our time," but toward a hegemonic war. I assume that the Clinton initiative constitutes a real policy alternative to start building a "regional concert" among China, the United States, Japan and other states in East Asia.[27]

Notes

1. Charles W. Kegley, Jr., and Eugene R. Wittkopf, *World Politics: Trends and Transformation* (fifth edition) (New York: St. Martin's Press), 1995 , p. 73; Sandra Suguwara, "Putting Their Eggs in a Massive Chinese Basket," *The Washington Post,* March 31, 1996; Michael Richardson, "U.S.-China-Japan Balance: Signs of Stress," *International Herald Tribune,* April 4, 1996; quoted from Kenneth Auchincloss, "Friend or Foe," *Newsweek,* April 1, 1996; Zakaria, "Is Realism Finished?" pp. 21-32.

2. See Taylor, *"Geopolitical World Order";* Taylor discusses four possible geopolitical orders as alternatives to the post-Cold War "unipolarity," which I find being over by the mid-1990s. There are a number of different scenarios in this respect available in the current literature of international relations. However, I find many of them disregard the rise of China. Johan Galtung, for example, is of the opinion that the world system may consist of three possible systems in the future: (1) rivalry among the ten biggest nations; (2) rivalry among three pan-regions; and (3) north-south conflict. See his *The True Worlds* (New York: Free Press), 1979.

3. Cohen, Geopolitics in the New World Era, pp. 18-23.

4. Ibid., p. 23.

5. The new geopolitics challenges in particular the deterministic (Wallerstein) and Long Cycle (Modelski) theories of the old geopolitics, which I dealt with earlier in this book.

6. The collapse of the Soviet Union had primarily domestic causes, which led to fundamental changes in the international system. See John Lewis Gaddis, "International Relations Theory and the End of the Cold War," *International Security,* No. 3, 1993, pp. 5-58; see also my *After the Cold War,* in which I dealt with the dynamism of the Cold War system.

7. Gregory Clark, "For East Asia, the Western Myth of Free Trade is a Good Joke," *International Herald Tribune,* August 15, 1996.

8. Cohen, "Geopolitics in the New World Era," p. 23.

9. C. Fred Bergsten, "Globalizing World Trade," *Foreign Affairs,* May/June 1996, pp. 105-120.

10. Ibid. See also "World Trade Overload?" *The Economist,* August 3, 1996. In 1996, China was not a member of the WTO, which already had 123 member-states.

11. See "EU Ready for New Trade Battle" in *International Herald Tribune,* July 25, 1996.

12. Carlisle, "Is the World Ready for Free Trade?"

13. Ibid.

14. Bergsten, "Globalizing World Trade," p. 105.

15. Calder, *Asia's Deadly Triangle,* p. 149; Lind, "Pax Atlantica," pp. 1-7.

16. Gaddis, *The United States and the End of the Cold War,* p. 5.

17. I have used Michael Mandelbaum (ed.), *The Strategic Quadrangle in East Asia,* (New York: Council on Foreign Relations Press), 1994. With respect to the evolution of Russia's role in world politics in the 1990s, see Alexander Rahr and Joachim Krause, *Russia's New Foreign Policy,* a study undertaken for the European Commission (Bonn: Research Institute of the German Society for Foreign Affairs), May 15, 1995.

18. Richard H. Salomon, "Who Will Shape the Emerging Structure of East Asia?" in Mandelbaum (ed.), *The Strategic Quadrangle in East Asia.*

19. Quoted in the *Nikkei Weekly,* May 22, 1995.

20. This view is shared by the majority of East Asian leaders. See Satoshi Isaka, "Japan is Urged to Back U.S. Presence in Asia," in Ibid.

21. John P. Ferriter, "Asia's Growing Oil Requirements," *International Herald Tribune,* August 19, 1996.

22. Calder, *Asia's Deadly Triangle,* pp. 220-221.

23. Mikhail Titarenko, "Asia-Pacific Nations Ready to Cooperate With Russia," *Trud,* July 10, 1996. Titarenko criticizes Russian authorities for their many

mistakes vis-a-vis Asia, particularly the decision to remain outside APEC.

24. However, Lind goes on to state that Japan's leaders are also not willing to act to contain China, either. Lind, "Pax Atlantica."

25. Ibid.

26. Salomon, "Who Will Shape the Emerging Structure of East Asia?"

27. I find the policy approach of the Clinton administration right and the only possible way of building a cooperative system in the region.

6

The Global Order for the 21st Century: Positive Interrelationship or Conflictual Rivalry?

A New Multipolar Order

"A transformation...from a unipolar to a bipolar system or from a bipolar to a multipolar system often will be closely associated with shifts in the strategies for peace fashioned by the leading contenders for power."
--Charles W. Kegley, Jr. and Gregory Raymond[1]

Have the conditions of the "long peace" that has obtained since the end of World War II vanished, or have additional conditions for peace emerged? "The end of World War II did not reduce insecurities--it ushered into being a period of chronic crisis, as the overkill produced an age of instability," as Charles Kegley states.[2] The period from 1945 to the present comprises the longest period of great-power peace since the birth of the modern (Westphalian) world system. In fact, the peak of the Westphalian era was reached with the end of the Cold War in the early 1990s. An ideological rivalry for hegemony between the world's two leading powers was fought without a military clash. Now, a window of opportunity for a lasting peace is open.

This book argues that the ongoing transition of the international system from the end of the post-Cold War short period of "unipolar momentum" toward new great power rivalry through a period of multipolar coexistence will contain a real chance to restructure the international system in order to avoid a potential military clash of emerging great powers in the early 21st century. This book makes the argument, however, that the "next rivalry," if it materializes, will have its geopolitical "meeting area" in East Asia and adjacent regions, such as the South China Sea.

One has to ask what are the necessary conditions of a lasting peace. Kenneth N. Waltz states in his 1979 *Theory of International Politics* that "international structure emerges from the interaction of states and then constrains them from taking certain actions while propelling them toward others."[3] I assume that states as such will remain the key actors in the system. Their position will be based, however, increasingly on their abilities to form and lead coalitions; thus, the dominant great powers will be leading states inside the emerging economic blocs. Furthermore, as the "unipolar momentum" has provided no substantial impetus for world government or other enduring and reliable institutions which could guarantee peace and security, the system as such remains anarchic and dangerous.

Yet, a specific great-power peace has lasted since the end of World War II, and one can discern some of the specific sources of this stability that has existed among between the present and emerging great powers, system or no. Across the span of nearly a half century of turbulent change in world politics, one constant has stood out: "There have been no wars among the 48 wealthiest countries in all that time."[4] In the middle of the 1990s, almost four billion of the world's population were living in states where market-friendly principles, albeit in different combinations, constituted the basis for economic policies. Rivalry based on ideological hegemony is perhaps gradually replaced with a rivalry based on economic prosperity.[5]

The emerging system of the "regional trading blocs" will, thus, be based on this promising layer of a globalized market economy. Only Africa seems to be left out. However, these blocs are compelled to watch their interests vis-a-vis each other from the security-political point of view as well. One of the underlying question marks will be whether they are able to avoid the return of power politics in their respective relations.

Basically, the European Westphalian system has become a global one. In this Westphalian system, it was possible to support conditions for peace, often for extended periods of time. At its most effective, it gave rise to the "concert system," which occurred only three times in modern history--from 1815 to 1854 or 1914, 1919 to 1920, and 1945 to 1946, as Robert Jervis reasoned in 1985. During the short period of "unipolar momentum," or "New World Order," one could argue that a global concert existed in 1989-1991.[6] Most recently, the 1995 Dayton accord on Bosnia cornerstoned a process which could conceivably evolve into a concert system later in the decade. However, the term "Concert of Europe" is often applied only to late 19th-century international politics, but the pursuit of self-interests was not sufficiently transformed to justify this label. The three 20th-century concerts were very brief, and one can argue that they did not really come into existence at all. At a minimum, there was a short period of extensive co-operation, and many statesmen and observers had at least some hopes for a longer-lasting arrangement.

During the Cold War era, peace was maintained to a large extent with military deterrence, not with co-operative means. One can argue that the Cold War peace was based primarily on the maintenance of balance of power. However, the end of the Cold War as such was not necessarily a result of deterrence but a combination of a number of factors, like an increase of economic interdependence, the advent of the communications revolution, and the spread of democratic values.[7]

As a consequence, the international system is undergoing a transition first from a brutal balance of power toward a concert. In a potentially new concert primarily involving the European Union, Russia, the United States, China and Japan, as well as their subordinates (allies), more emphasis is, thus, given to co-operative means than to the military balance of power (deterrence). They are also increasingly bound by systemic factors, like the globalization of market economy, shared threats posed by security risks, and communications.

I assume that although we live in a global system, we may be unable to establish a particular world order or world concert to safeguard peace universally. All security arrangements will probably remain regional or, at best, continental in nature. It is another question, however, if there will emerge a possibility to establish a number of regional arrangements which together could constitute a world concert for the maintenance of peace worldwide. In reference to the "depressed mood" that was perceived after the Persian Gulf war, Stanley Hoffman of Harvard University writes that "the problem of order has become even more complex than before."[8] Hoffman, as many other prominent scholars, has set very high standards for order in the world community. I am sure, however, that we have to accept more turbulence and even global "disorder" but will still find it a system where we are able to avoid major wars. We have to accept a dangerous peace (such as the one reached in Dayton) as a reality in order to avoid the worst-case scenario.

It seems to be one of the new realities that a co-operative security system, although fragile, was established between Russia and the Euro-Atlantic states as a result of the Organization of Security and Cooperation in Europe (OSCE) and other security arrangements in the course of the post-Cold War period of "unipolarity." This system will remain a subject of tests for years to come. However, a real chance for the emergence of a security space and collective security system consisting of the OSCE states can be expected to emerge in the late 1990s. This means that a "long peace" may continue from the middle of the 1990s until 2010, particularly in the Euro-Atlantic and Eurasian spheres .[9]

For the first time in the history of mankind, a really global multipolar international system is looming on the horizon, not so much a validation of Kant but rather because the technological and communications revolutions permit us--even force us--to work together vis-a-vis problems that have no sympathy for national or even regional boundaries. However, even in this "defensive globalization," there will be regions. My aim is first to shed light theoretically on what are the prospects of peace within the system transformation from the emerging multipolarity toward a possible new bipolarity consisting of a Euro-Atlantic bloc and an Asian bloc. The question is how to strengthen multipolar peace instead of military competition within this system; in other words, it would be wise to plan how to avoid a dangerous type of multipolarity.

In the 1990s, the debate has intensified about which type of power distribution--unipolar, bipolar, or multipolar--is the most stable and, as a consequence, creates the "healthiest" system. Most scholars agree that world order does not spring up organically, but rather is deliberately made up by its leading powers. Concern about a multipolar future stems from the fact that when power has been evenly distributed

among several great powers in the past, they have tended to act asser-
tively, independently, and competitively. "Conceivably, a new
multipolar distribution of power could culminate in a renewed struggle
for supremacy that could end the longest period of great-power peace
in modern history," as Kegley and Raymond have reasoned.[10]
On the one hand, I assume that within the emerging multipolarity
the prospects for a global concert--and peace--are promising. "In the
context of the global forces unleashed in the past 50 years, only a collective effort can give states the framework and the strength to shape
their own destiny in the promising but turbulent times lie ahead," as
the *Report of the Independent Working Group on the Future of the
United Nations* concludes.[11] On the other hand, as Henry Kissinger
reasons, "History so far has shown us only two roads to international
stability: domination or equilibrium."[12] If no unit (state or politico-
economic bloc) is able to dominate and the dispersion of power
continues, the prospects for peace undoubtedly will be affected. Is
peace less probable than war?
I have argued that the collapsed bipolar "cold war world" was, as an
international system, dangerous and "sick." The threat of global nuclear destruction as posed by the Cold War has receded. We have certainly witnessed how the community of nations can benefit when the
interests of major powers converge on global peace. We are moving,
as U.S. Deputy Secretary of State Lawrence Eagleburger proclaimed in
1989, "into...a world in which power and influence is diffused among
a multiplicity of states--[a] multipolar world." One can ask two questions:

1. Is this new emerging multipolar system comparable with the previous multilateral systems?
2. Is a multipolar system safer and better than the unipolar or bipolar systems?

One cannot compare the emerging multipolar order with any of the
previous ones in history. I will argue, however, that the number of its
units (five or six) and its size (global) indicate that it could become a
rather stable system. It seems to be a widely agreed view that because
there is no "real consensus on whether systems with a certain number

of poles (uni-, bi- or multipolar) are more war prone than others," it would be imprudent to jump to the conclusion that a new multipolar system will necessarily spell out another period of warfare.

Yet the logic of realpolitik argues that the probability of collision increases as the number of units (in this case, great powers) increases. System size is assumed to make a difference in the degree to which great-power interactions are conflictual or cooperative. How does size affect stability of the system? R. Harrison Wagner, for example, argues that multipolar systems with three great-power contestants are the most stable, whereas Arthur Lee Burns maintains that "the most stable arrangement would seem to be a world of five or some greater odd number of powers, independent and of approximately equal strength." The size of the system is also a function of whether it is a regional or global arrangement, not only simply of the number of its units.[13]

The largest multipolar system (1815-1919) was the longest lasting and among the least prone to experience great-power wars. The smallest system, with the shortest duration (1492-1521), experienced five great-power wars. In short, the number of great-power competitors may matter, but not decisively. However, rapid changes in the rank order of units of the system can easily create anxiety. By the mid-1990s, the continuing decline and disintegration of Russia and the continuing rise and "unification" of China constitute the most dramatic change factors in the system.

From the point of view of system stability and peace, not only the number of units and the size of the system are crucial. I assume that the "systemic stability" has to be added, particularly as the structural conditions of peace have gained ground dramatically in the post-Cold War era. The majority of the powers of the emerging multipolarity are entities strongly committed to democracy and market economy. Democracy has not yet rooted in China, but has taken major steps in Russia. Consequently, this expanding synergy of democratic values, and their impact on the structure of the international system, may strengthen the conditions of peace decisively in the late 1990s and early 21st century.[14]

In addition to the emerging power poles, sub-structures of new divisions also exist on the globe. Since the old divisions between East and West--and, to some degree, North and South as well--have to a great extent faded away, new cultural, economic, environmental and social divisions will emerge. In order to generalize the development, some scholars speak about the post-Cold War world divided into a zone of stability and into a zone of turmoil. Although this scenario would be at least partly true, I assume that the real power poles will remain the most important factors influencing the basic structure of the international system.[15]

The belief that democratic policy-making institutions will produce peace follows the idealist convictions of 18th century philosopher Immanuel Kant in his text *Perpetual Peace*, namely that democracies are inherently less warlike than autocracies. After the Cold War, scholars take the consequences of democratization more seriously, because they have discovered that

> Although preventive war has been preferred response of declining authoritarian leaders, no democracy has ever initiated such a war. Instead, depending on the regime type of the rising challenger, democratic states have chosen accommodation, defensive alliances, or internal balancing.[16]

Simply put, democracies have dealt with conflicts against other democracies by methods other than war.

To a degree, the end of the Cold War rivalry enhanced the capacity of multilateral organizations to resolve civil and interstate conflicts. In particular, in the years 1989-92 the management of conflict became "a growth industry." In 1992, the United States presidential campaign was influenced by return of a more neo-Wilsonian view of international politics. Western policy makers often claimed that the institutions that "served the West well before the Soviet Union collapsed must only be reshaped to encompass Eastern Europe as well." Yet there are a number of influential voices which claim that one has to be careful with "the false promise of international institutions."[17] Irrespective of point of view, it seems incontrovertible that the new security risks do make it necessary to enhance collective efforts. The real question arises whether there are genuine opportunities for *global governance*? Is it possible to rely basically upon the body of multilateral organizations for controlling change peacefully?

Multilateral organizations--most of which were substantially affected by the Cold War conditions--were designed for specific purposes. The multilateral system as it appears today represents an assortment of intergovernmental structures and institutions, comprising the UN and its system, financial institutions--including the Bretton Woods institutions World Bank and International Monetary Fund (IMF)--regional organizations, and a host of other international organizations. While some multilateral organizations are not universal in terms of membership, they may nevertheless be global in terms of their interests, outreach and ramifications of action. As Adries van Agt puts it, "The present organizational overload in the international global system needs to be pruned so as to enable leaders committed to global cooperation to focus on the truly important issues and to choose the most suitable organization for action."[18]

In its 1995 report, the Yale Group posited that no enhancements in the effectiveness of global governance will compensate for the absence in a country of good domestic governance, a healthy social fabric, and decent living standards. But the group affirmed that if nation-states are to handle global challenges of the type listed above, they need help. The issue then becomes how to organize this "help" collectively, such as through the United Nations, the regional organizations, and other multilateral instruments. Undoubtedly, these actions do not entirely replace the instruments of equilibrium. Yet the multilateral instruments should be developed strong enough to substitute for, or at least combine with, domination and equilibrium as security strategies.

Besides the expansion of systemic factors--democracy, market economy and social security--the great power relationships as well as the interests of the great powers to develop multilateral institutions together, therefore, constitute the framework for an improved international system. If so, then the issue becomes one of sequencing: will today's great powers be able to establish first a more lasting concert among themselves and then move towards a collective security system in the "Wilsonian spirit"? By the mid-1990s, there existed at least a "passive" global concert which made it possible to delimit and constrain regional conflicts, as in the former Yugoslavia and in the Caucasus. However, a more "active" concert is needed for getting these and other conflicts solved in the future. The international community should move from a concert to collective security modes, which can be seen as a more inclusive form of concert.[19]

The UN organization has been subject of paradoxical development. On the one hand, it has become clear that the great powers have remained rather reluctant to pay for any substantial expansion of UN conflict-management responsibilities and other activities related to the strengthening of the UN as a body of collective security. Global recession has had even worse effect on resources available for conflict-management activities. "In the post-Cold War context, governing elites and publics seek to divert expenditure from foreign policy and security tasks to long-postponed domestic economic and social needs."[20] On the other hand, the world organization has gradually provided a strengthened basis for an intensive development of international law. Indeed, through a series of global conferences, "it moved toward an international consensus on global problems like the environment, population, the status of women, human rights, development, and many other basic issues."[21] The main problem seems to be, however, the continuing change of the international system, which seems to be faster than the ability of the international community to devise and respond with creative solutions. This creates options for an increase of unilateral actions in world politics. Unfortunately, even an improved international system is bound to contain major flaws and sources of uncertainty and instability, any or all of which could render the attempt to develop a set of rules quixotic.

Prospects for Global Governance

"If we do not find the vision and the leadership to defeat the unprecedented new security threats of global climate change, ozone depletion, habitat destruction and desertification, then those threats may well defeat us."
                                                                    --Bill Clinton

"Environmental trends are becoming a major force that could alter the very foundations of the international political system in the coming decades. Some will result in changes that are sudden and dramatic, like the Antarctic ozone hole. Others will result in changes that are slow and underreported, but nevertheless profound and irreversible, like the projected

flooding of coastal areas from sea-level rise and the growing volume of en
vironmental refugees crossing national borders."

--Jim MacNeill[22]

This book deals with power, its relations, its derivatives, its distribution and its scope in world politics. However, the world faces threats that are of a structural nature and which affect the whole global community rather than only certain states or groups. Population growth--if unchecked--could dramatically change the world by destroying the environment and by mass migration of unprecedented scale. Even absent such population pressures, ecological problems as such threaten the whole globe, or at least require globally-coordinated solutions.

I have no hope or intention of analyzing these global challenges thoroughly. Rather, within the scope of this book it should be asked how different kinds of international systems affect the management of these problems. It could be even asked which international system is the best for addressing these common threats.

Preserving peace is the sine qua non of coping with these problems. In this view also, rivalry is better than war. While the impact of these new nonmilitary threats to global welfare are potent, this does not, however, mean that geoeconomics or ecopolitics will replace geopolitics.[23] The power-political system defines the constraints and room for action of global politics and global policies.

The period of the end of the Cold War--the unipolar New World Order--was over by the middle of the 1990s. In theory, it could have been quite effective in dealing with common challenges. One paramount leader would show the way and do the action, while others would follow under the umbrella of international organizations like the United Nations. It was certainly a more effective idea for dealing with new kinds of problems, as in the predecessor bipolar system there was by definition a basic disagreement on what constituted a fair way to organize the world.

Regardless of its merits, it is clear that the New World Order has collapsed. I assume that in the nascent "post-New World Order," an emerging multipolar system characterized by strengthening rivalry will last until 2010-2020 and then be challenged by a new division of the world. Consequently, I am sceptical about the ability of a multipolar system to deal with grave global problems if the relations of the central actors are conflictual or intensely competitive.

In contrast with the multipolar systems or orders of the 19th century and before, the coming multipolarity will be characterized by a global economic foundation. The first criteria of a Kantian eternal peace has been fulfilled.[24] Unfortunately, the second Kantian criteria, a global democratic space, remains far from fulfillment, and the third, realization that war is too destructive to remain an instrument of politics, borders on fantasy.

With the collapse of the Soviet geostrategic realm, the UN no longer poses a diplomatic threat to the West, and to the US in particular. One would therefore expect that the US would pay more attention to the opportunities afforded by the world organization, perhaps building on the fig leaf it provided early in the decade for the American-led drive against Saddam Hussein. Sadly, the opposite is true. The reduction of the role and status of the UN has continued apace during the mid-1990s, lamentably as a function of US opposition to any real enhancing of its writ. Additionally, in the words of Swedish diplomat Jan Eliasson,

> The United Nations has not recovered from the setbacks suffered in Somalia, Rwanda and former Yugoslavia. The United Nations saves lives every day with its humanitarian and development programs and successful peacekeeping operations. It remains unique as an instrument for finding global solutions to global problems. *But it is not performing to capacity. It suffers from bureaucratic inertia.*[25] (emphasis added)

The United Nations and other institutional actors of the world community have to cope with emerging global security challenges: containment of the population explosion and promotion of sustainable human development. The almost geometric dynamism of the population explosion may end up suffocating one national economy after another, gradually forcing ecological burnout on a global scale, accelerating the greenhouse effect with devastating sea level rise and loss of agricultural lands, and triggering considerable population movements. The spiral of ever more poverty, disease and conflicts will intensify. For example, China will likely face both a shortage of food resources and a deterioration of its environment simultaneously in the 1990s. These factors may push China to follow a more aggressive policy vis-a-vis its neighbors, virtually none of whom it gets along with already.

The UN could function as an international tool to fight global problems. This is, however, not up to the UN itself but rather depends on a broad consensus of its members. Therefore the UN--or any other global forum--depends on the nature and structure of the international system at hand. It is the only really global political forum available to manage change between the emerging political trading blocs and the rest of the world. But it is clear that the UN was a success between 1945 and 1989 insofar as the superpowers allowed it to be. The brief unipolar interlude in 1989-1991 saw efficient use of the UN in the Gulf War. The power relations characterizing the coming multipolarity, no less than those of the recently passed bipolarity and unipolarity, will determine the effectiveness and scope of global organizations just as much as they did in the Cold War and New World Order.

The institutional premises for coping with the emerging new rivalry are confusing. One can state that the global system will not by necessity become more effective through a broader involvement of regional organizations. Such institutions are frequently weaker in performance and decision-making capabilities than the United Nations, and are on even shakier grounds as regards their financial basis. It is of crucial importance, however, to promote regional arrangements for maintaining stability and peace. I concur with the diagnosis-cum-prescription that regionalism might be useful for specific circumstances but can never serve as a general recipe for pursuing world governance and order. Instead, all efforts should be undertaken to enhance cohesion and the efficiency of global cooperation and interdependence and to avoid a splitting up into regional groupings. The fact is, however, that regional centers of gravity make it imperative to work for cooperative security arrangements among these powers both through the United Nations and among themselves.[26]

The situation differs in the various regions of the globe. In Europe, a well-established structure exists through NATO (and its recent Partnership for Peace arrangements), the European Union, the Western European Union and the OSCE. But even with all these trappings, Europe cannot deal effectively with its own security challenges. Regardless of the Dayton accord or any solution that eventually quells the on-going conflict in the Balkans, the word "Bosnia" will mock Europe's (and, for that matter, the West's) claim to successful post-Cold War transition. In Asia and the Pacific, no regional organizations exist which could assume a role in peace-keeping or conflict resolution. This reflects to some extent a historically greater reliance on global multilateral institutions. In Africa, the Organization for African Unity (OAU) is evolving, but it will not be capable of carrying out any large-scale peace-keeping operation without asssistance from outside. The democratization of southern Africa has simply shifted the focus of the continent's destabilization northward. Nigeria, despite being one of the most advanced African countries, presents one of the continent's most perplexing security challenges. Meanwhile, many more tragedies like those in Somalia, Liberia, Burundi and Rwanda are looming. To ward them off, some preventive, low-key and non-military intervention should be initiated, containing conflicts before they degenerate into wholesale violence. Elsewhere, the Middle East faces the particular problem of Islamic fundamentalism, which is unlikely to be solved by any regional organization. In Latin America, the experience of the last several decades has been mixed. Domestically, if you will, democrati-zation and economic liberalization have progressed within many of the region's countries, but regionally, the Organization of American States (OAS) has been irrelevant with respect to important issues. As a re-sult, informal and ad hoc groupings were formed, such as the Conta-dora Group, the Group of Eight later transformed into the Rio Group. These smaller scale cooperative groupings present a viable framework that may in time evolve into larger regional cooperation. It may be that, for all or several of these regions, cooperation--institutional or otherwise--will only succeed if it is issue-specific.

The international order of the early 21st century will most likely be principally a balance of power system among five global powers: the United States, the European Union, Russia, China and Japan. All of them will be challenged by a number of security threats and risks: Is-lam against Russia and the European Union (not to mention the "Great Satan," the US), Russia against the US and China in nuclear terms, and internal revolts against central authority in China and Russia.

Due to its increasing economic resources and power-political position, China will be the most central actor to this emerging multipolar security (dis)order. It follows, then, that the relationship between China and Russia is perhaps the most interesting and crucial tie in the future international order of New Rivalry. If they join forces, the center of gravity of world politics will definitively shift to the Asian heartland. If they remain divided, the maritime powers will have an easier task in containing their continental opponents.

Despite their economic eminence, the German-centered European Union and Japan will be modest actors in the international order of New Rivalry. The status of Japan, in particular, depends on the balance between China and the United States. Many commentators have predicted the strategic rise of Japan. In my view, Japan is condemned to be shadowed by China; the island nation is beset by strategic weaknesses such that it could never comprehensively challenge China and win--a global economic powerhouse, definitely, but also a power-political pygmy. It should either stay allied with the United States, shift its allegiance to China, or seek strategic neutrality and hope that political restraint and a commensurate military capability will keep it clear of conflicts with other great(er) powers.

The position of the European Union is similar to that of Japan. Not capable of challenging either Russia or the United States, it has to find a modus vivendi in the balance of power between the two powers. Thus its options are similar to Japan's: It must either ally itself with one or remain neutral. In reality, however, Europe's choice was made long ago. The real discussion at this point regards modalities: The transatlantic relationship is crucial for Europeans, even though the future will probably see the degeneration of NATO (probably more in purpose than in structure) and its replacement with a new kind of transatlantic partnership. A trilateral arrangement among the United States, Europe and Russia should be instituted (if not necessarily institutionalized) to manage orderly change in Europe.

Prospects for a New Division of the World

"The 21st century is apt to be one where there is a definite economic leader but not a century where one country towers above all the rest... America

will be the military superpower of the 21st century. But that, if anything, gives it a handicap in its attempts to remain an economic superpower in the 21st century."

--Lester Thurow

"During the bipolar Cold War, the leaders of each bloc tried to destroy and revolutionize their rivals and sought to wear down the other by using force to maintain and expand their blocs."

--Stephen Pelz

"The Alliance must embrace innovation or risk relevance....The January [1994] summit [opens] the door to an evolutionary process of NATO expansion. The process should be nondiscriminatory and inclusive."

--Warren Christopher[27]

Since the mid-1990s, the world system has been increasingly a multipolar one. I assume, however, that it will be challenged by trends toward a more bipolar type of system in the early 21st century--an Asian system versus the Euro-Atlantic system. Consequently, no stability is possible, although a major war between the participants of this multipolar concert must be ruled out. In the present multipolarity, we can expect the major powers to fear each other and align with or oppose each other in particular issue-areas, as interests dictate. Under conditions of multipolarity, there are no permanent allies; rather, alliances are based on short-term convergences of interest--"they are marriages of convenience."[28]

We will face, then, a transition from the existing fragile multipolarity to something else, primarily a kind of new bipolarity. As I have argued, multipolarity generally presages the alignment of former adversaries. China will challenge the US, at least in East Asia, and, as a result, globally. The question will be who will align with whom and take the leadership initiative in either the multipolar or bipolar milieus described herein.

In the following I briefly try to elaborate the problem. A more lengthy assessment would go beyond the scope of the present volume.

We are puzzling with the emerging mental maps of the world system in the times ahead. I have taken the view that the present complex system of nation-states will be replaced with groupings of such states inside economic spaces, or blocs. This emerging structure of trading blocs will have its flaws, of course, although in the final analysis, this basic structure does not change as a result. And even these flaws strengthen the argument that the old nation-state could become obsolete as a result of systemic change.

I want to illustrate these flaws with the analysis by Riccardo Petrella, the official futurist of the European Union.[29] In his view, we may face two such mental maps of the future world system. One map is that of a world dominated by a hierarchy of 30 city-regions linked more to each other than to those territorial hinterlands to which the nation-state once bound them. This wealthy archipelago of city-regions-- with manageable populations of 8 million-12 million--will be run by an alliance between the global merchant class and metropolitan governments whose chief function is supporting the competitiveness of the global firms to which they are host. These disassociated islands (city-regions) will be surrounded by an impoverished lumpenplanet (uprooted peasants, migrants, homeless etc.). Of the eight billion people expected to populate the earth by 2020, five billion will live in Asia, and, of this, one billion will reside 50 cities with more than 20 million inhabitants each.

The other map pictures the global civil society that has emerged with the information age in all the major city-regions linked together across fading national boundaries, balancing the myopic commercialism of the merchant class with a global social contract. Instead of a world where the purely competitive or merely fortunate are forced to hole up in gated city-regions for fear of the crime and pandemonium all about them, the order based on a global contract would give rise to a vital, multicultural civilization on a planetary scale. "A kind of plural, global agora rather than the mediaeval moated castle" would symbolize this new civilization. This agora, or global civil society, would be the interlinkage between local territoriality and the consciousness of the first planetary generation, "the first generation with a global dimension," as Petrella concludes in his analysis.

These two dimensions of the ongoing system change should be kept in mind when pondering over my basic theses about the trading blocs and their security-political repercussions. Perhaps one of the key questions about world politics in the 21st century is the relationship between economics and politics--separated or intertwined? Economic actors--city-regions, groupings of nation-states or old superpowers--have outgrown the constraints of previous "geopolitical states." They have acquired a large degree of autonomy from those states and are no longer hostages to previous political power calculations. The relationship between new economic and old political actors is a combination of autonomy and interaction. Both influence each other. They form two partially overlapping entities.

The Westphalian state-system has become global at the same time that it has obsolesced. Territorial political actors cover the whole globe but have lost full control over the territories that once defined them.

World politics evolves on a continuum of cooperation - competition - rivalry - conflict. The end of the bipolar division of power gave way for a short space of international cooperation, a US-centered unipolar world order which proved to be of an infinitely short duration. Economic competition will increase and the world is likely to evolve into competing trade blocs, which challenge each other.

The economic blocs, a trilateral world, will give space to a new rivalry, a multipolar balance of forces--a latter-day Concert of Europe, only now on a global scale. In this order, China will be central, while the United States, Russia, the European Union and--most of all--Japan will have to find their place in a world increasingly centered on Chinese might. The seminal preoccupation of this system will be how to prevent this rivalry from degenerating into military conflict.

China's size, coupled with its economic growth rate, is bound to produce the world leader, provided that central control can keep its grip on dynamic regional entities. Moreover, China is already developing a strategic capability and will soon be able to exert itself in the Pacific and Asia. It could be said that China will be an imperial state in the new system of world politics. By imperial, I mean that its economic might will be used for political ends, the translation of the *influence* it has always had into a *power* extending beyond its geographic borders. This is a break with recent Chinese history, and clearly owes little to Mao Zedong and his followers, who were by and large content with ideological deference rather than force projection.

Russia's relationship with China will prove crucial to the future world order. Will China and Russia provide a new cold war, a standstill between two great continental powers, or will they find mutual understanding to the detriment of others? Because Russia finds its security anxieties on its southern and eastern borders rather than its western ones, any relationship between it and China is bound to be complicated by what could be charitably termed "geopolitical sensitivities." Many years will have to pass before the Russo-Chinese frontier is as permeable and peaceful as the US-Canadian one, and even more before Russia and China could plausibly claim a congruence of interest similar to that exhibited by the two North American countries. This could be a favorable omen for Western Europe's relations with Russia.

The United States will probably be a passive but important force in the global balance--its military capability and strategic focus should keep China balanced in the Pacific and Russia balanced in Europe. Japan's and Western Europe's prosperity depends on the United States' willingness and capacity to fulfill this balancing role. Although the United States is likely to remain a more inward-looking power than it was from roughly the end of the Second World War to the end of the Cold War, it will also remain as continent-sized balancer to China and Russia, inheritor of the mantle Great Britain wore for many years in regard to Europe.

World politics in the 21st century will have no single leading state-- no state will be able to stand alone against an alliance of other great powers. Machtpolitik, the distribution of global power and capability, will still be the central element of world politics. Economic prowess is critical, but will never of itself permit Europe (broadened, deepened or otherwise) or Japan from dominating the global system.

Power politics and the balance of power between great powers are, however, unable to solve some of the great problems of the international system: poverty, ecologic instability, the rapidly increasing population. Other systems will have to be devised, cooperative arrangements that give due respect to political realities (national and otherwise) and that take into account the constraints of the new rivalry.

The close link between Western Europe and the United States is likely to survive. While NATO, the Cold War expression of solidarity, may not ultimately survive the transition from bipolarity to new rivalry intact, a new transatlantic partnership will take shape. Europe and America will still share a common strategic commitment, but the responsibilities and rights in the grouping will be divided in a novel way.

Russia will most probably find a new cooperative relationship with Western Europe, combining its own resources and European know-how on a new scale. Western Europe will no longer be a threat but a partner to Russia, provided that sensible leadership remains in power in the latter.

If transatlantic partnership remains central to the Western order and Russia develops a cooperative relationship with the West, then the world system of the 21st century will develop some aspects of a new bipolar balance of power with a Western sphere opposed to a Chinese sphere. Japan's place in such a system remains open, but only to a degree. In a multipolar setting it would be free to choose between several masters, but in a bipolar one it is too near to China to be able to resist its strong gravitational pull.

Notes

1. Kegley and Raymond, *A Multipolar Peace,* p. 150.

2. Charles W. Kegley, "Explaining Great-Power Peace: The Sources of Prolonged Postwar Stability," in Kegley, (ed.), *The Long Postwar Peace* (New York: HarperCollins), 1991, pp.3-22.

3. Kenneth N. Waltz, *Theory of International Politics* (Wesley, MA: Addison Publishers), 1979.

4. John Mueller, "Dropping Out of the War Systems," *The Los Angeles Times,* September 12, 1988.

5. This book does not deal in detail with the sources of "long peace" but wants to stress the historic logic of the theses of Immanuel Kant concerning the conditions of lasting peace. Kant believed that the combination of representative government and the painful lessons of recurrent warfare would eventually lead to perpetual peace. On the foundations of international security in the post-Cold War international environment in "Kantian" terms, see Michael Mandelbaum, *The Dawn of Peace in Europe* (New York: Twentieth Century Fund), 1996, pp. 77, 125-126.

6. Robert Jervis, "From Balance to Concert: A Study of International Security Cooperation", *World Politics*, October 1985, pp. 58-79. The last concert emerged after the writing of Jervis' paper.

7. See my *After the Cold War*.

8. Stanley Hoffman, "Delusions of World Order," *New York Review of Books*, April 9, 1992, p. 42. Hoffman's article is critically analyzed by Singer and Wildavsky, *The Real World Order*, pp. 190-193.

9. It is my firm view that Russia and the Euro-Atlantic states do not want to solve their problems by military means, although a number of local conflicts will continue to take place in the former Yugoslavia and in the Caucasus region, for example. See my *After the Cold War*.

10. Since the birth of the modern state system in the late 15th century, there have been six periods of multipolarity: 1495-1521; 1604-1618; 1648-1702; 1713-1792; 1815-1914; and 1919-1939 (the latter period perhaps not coincidentally providing the timeframe and title reference for E.H. Carr's classic realist study of international relations, *The Twenty Years' Crisis*).

11. *A Report of the Independent Working Group on the Future of the United Nations* (Yale University and the Ford Foundation; June 19, 1995).

12. Henry Kissinger, "Balance of Power Sustained," in Graham Allison and Gregory Treverton, (eds.), *Rethinking America's Security: Beyond Cold War to New World Order* (New York: Norton), 1992.

13. A large number of investigations suggest that a direct relationship between multipolar systems and the probability of war cannot be drawn. See, for example, Bruce Bueno Mesquita, *The War Trap* (New Haven, CT: Yale University Press), 1981; Jack S. Levy, "Polarity of the System and International Stability: An Empirical Analysis," in Alan Ned Sabrosky (ed.), *Polarity and War* (Boulder, CO: Westview Press), 1985; Harrison R. Wagner, "The Theory of Games and the Balance of Power," *World Politics*, July 1986; and Arthur Lee Burns, *Of Powers and Their Politics* (Englewood Cliffs, NJ: Prentice-Hall), 1964.

14. Democracy has been growing throughout the globe since the 1980s. On December 31, 1991, *The Wall Street Journal*, citing a Freedom House report, estimated that at that moment 41% of the world's population lived in "free" countries, 37% lived in "partly-free" countries, and 22% lived in "non-free" countries. One can expect that China's further development, if towards democracy, will be one of the major turning points on the road toward a global democratic space in the early 21st century.

15. See, for example, Singer and Wildavsky's work on "the two zones" in *The Real World Order*, cited earlier.

16. See Randall L. Schweller, "Domestic Structure and Preventive War," *World Politics*, January 1992, pp. 235-269; also, Michael W. Doyle, "Liberalism

and World Politics Revisited," in Charles W. Kegley (ed.), *Controversies in International Relations Theory: Realism and Neoliberal Challenge* (New York: St. Martin's Press), 1995, pp. 83-106.

17. John J. Mearsheimer, "The False Promise of International Institutions," *International Security*, Winter 1994/95, pp. 5-49.

18. For in-depth analysis of global multilateral organizations, see the May 1994 draft paper of the High Level Group (chaired by van Agt) on the future role of global multilateral organizations cited in the previous chapter.

19. In this respect, the Concert of Europe was organized to deal with the early 19th century set of collective fears.

20. S. Neil MacFarlane and Thomas. G. Weiss, "Regional Organizations and Regional Security," *Security Studies*, Autumn 1992, pp. 6-37.

21. The Report of the Yale Working Group referred to above presents, for example, the idea of a "Global Alliance for Sustainable Development" within the framework of the United Nations. Regardless of the merits of this particular proposition, such perspectives are necessary to develop "concert structures" in the multipolar system.

22. Both cited in Jim MacNeill, "Ecogeopolitics After Rio," in Hans d'Orville (ed.), *Perspectives of Global Responsibility* (New York: InterAction Council), 1993.

23. See Kegley and Raymond, *A Multipolar Peace?*

24. Concerning the Kantian world order, see my "Is This the Chance for a New Euro-Atlantic Alliance?" in Ian M. Cuthbertson, (ed.), *Redefining the CSCE* (New York and Helsinki: Institute for EastWest Studies and Finnish Institute of International Affairs), 1992, pp. 69-91.

25. Jan Eliasson, "A United Nations to Heal and Link the Nations," *International Herald Tribune*, September 4, 1996.

26. See Rosemary Righter, *Utopia Lost: The United Nations and World Order,* (New York: Twentieth Century Fund), 1995, p. 372.

27. Thurow, *Head to Head,* p. 246; Stephen Pelz, "Changing International Systems, The World Balance of Power, and the United States: 1776-1976," *Diplomatic History,* Winter 1991, pp. 47-81; US Secretary of State Warren Christopher, February 1994.

28. Charles W. Kegley, Jr., "Does the US Have a Role in the Future European Security System?" in Cuthbertson (ed.), *Redefining the CSCE*, pp. 111-144.

29. Petrella, "A Global Agora vs. Gated City-Regions."

7

Constructing the Real Future

"Opinions differ on why the third hegemonic war of the twentieth century ended without mass destruction. The conclusions reached do matter, for the inferences drawn are certain to affect leaders' thinking about how to manage great-power rivalries in the future."

--Charles W. Kegley, Jr. and Eugene Wittkopf

"In the past, deeds drove words. A hardheaded reading of reality was seen to require certain politics...Today words are driving deeds. Rhetorical devices--terms like 'leadership,' 'credibility,' 'engagement,' 'sole remaining superpower,' 'moral ascendancy,' and 'American values'-- have taken on a life of their own, a virtual reality that prompts policy decisions separate from any calculation of American interests."

--Jonathan Clarke[1]

The conventional wisdom that wishful thinking pervades political decision making is not supported, as Robert Jervis puts it, by the evidence from either experimental or natural settings, but rather

...Statesmen sometimes see what they want to see, but whether this error is more common than the opposite one or more frequent than would be expected by chance and non-affective variables has yet to be demonstrated....[indeed] desires and fears have most impact when perceptions matter least. Woodrow Wilson had to decide to ask for a declaration of war against Germany. He had to do this although in his thinking the world was moving away from the era of war. Wilson was of the opinion that he did not have any alternative, no choice but to declare war.[2]

We are facing a similar kind of puzzle in the late 1990s and on into the early 21st century. Do we have an alternative to the emergence of an eternal rivalry between great powers and, possibly, war? While we currently experience peace in the fragile multipolar international system, it is one fraught with danger that may last for decades to come.

Thus, the peaceful end of the Cold War did not ensure a peaceful future, any more than did the "Great War" (World War I), America's entry into which Wilson justified by calling it "the war to end all wars." As I have argued in this volume, the insights given us by long-cycle theory might leave us understandably thinking that the prevailing trends in the diffusion of economic power will lead to renewed cycles of competition, rivalry, conflict and perhaps even war among the great powers, and that the range of new problems and potential threats will expand. Instability will primarily, but not entirely, result from the changes unfolding in the international system's structure. As contending powers arise, a new multipolar structure will emerge.

What's more, one can say that a profound disparity is already defining itself between the strategic and economic rank-orders of the major powers. The strategic hierarchy in a six-power central balance would still commence with the US, followed by Russia, the European Union, China, India and, last, Japan. Economically, however, the EU is first, as it is approximately 30% larger than runner-up US, followed by Japan, China, India and finally Russia.[3]

Throughout history, changes in comparative economic advantage have preceded changes in political advantage. As economic rivals have struggled to protect their wealth and compete for position, political conflicts--often escalating to military confrontation--have often resulted. Can China achieve what it needs without flexing its military muscles? Certainly not. Can the United States protect its global interests without military intervention? An equally emphatic "no."

Concerning political actors, I assume that the economic hierarchy will gradually dictate the strategic rank-order. The question is how the emerging political trading blocs, then, will behave. Will they be able to avoid military conflicts among themselves (as opposed to conflict between individual blocs and other, less important actors)? I believe that the new political actors want to avoid a hegemonic war because they understand that any such military exchange fought with latter-day arsenals would cause the end of our civilization. Whether this realization will automatically prompt cooperative tendencies, however, is another issue.

Immanuel Kant and Woodrow Wilson both believed that democracies were not warlike because war never served the interests of the public as a whole; when the public could check the wishes of the rulers, it would therefore prevent bellicose behavior. We cannot take democracy for granted, however, as it has both its economic and political foundations. Are the democracies going to be in a hegemonic position in the emerging system? Or is one of the less democratic new political trading blocs willing to challenge the multipolar order, which is in fact an order of democratic hegemony. In the following, I try to conclude this volume by casting light on the problem of the "social construction" of reality, which I believe is critical to the maintenance of peace.

The Social Construction of the Real Future

In the following, I try to draw some "pre-theoretical" conclusions based primarily on "constructivism." The reason is that in today's post-Cold War world, global communication and its related factors stimulate conditions for the importance of "social construction" of reality more than ever before in mankind's history. By the mid-1990s, no new world order had emerged, although when the leaders and other influential players of the international system discussed the possible future, they nevertheless spoke about common values leading to collective actions and interests. They also spoke about emerging threats and new divisions among themselves. A worldwide rhetorical process of words was gradually creating a particular future: a reality on the basis of which the competing great powers would make concrete policy decisions later on.

The Cold War was primarily a conflict between two evolved versions of progressivism--socialism and neoclassical capitalism. Furthermore, there existed almost no real interaction or accommodation (that is to say, no real interdependence) between these two "civilizations." As Eisuke Sakakibara reasons, "Both ideologies set a rapid increase and fair distribution of material welfare as their goal. According to socialists, the way to achieve such a goal is state planning; according to neoclassicists, the market."[4]

A major difference between the Cold War and the emerging multi-polar system is that there exists deepening interaction between the key powers of the latter one. Consequently, a new world system consist-ing of competing economic-political blocs is also being socially con-structed through "intersubjective systemic structures."

Basically, one can make one important distinction between the ac-tors of the multipolar blocs: whether they base their analysis and pol-icy on egoistic or collective identity. Does the emerging bloc system provide durable conditions for inter-bloc cooperation or hardening competition? The US may have major difficulties redefining its iden-tity in this system in any event, but will it attempt that redefinition through new threats and enemies or through collective identity (as, for example, through the United Nations or NAFTA). The same kind of questions can be asked in regard to Russia and China.

Leading constructivist Alexander Wendt emphasizes that there exists a real window of opportunity for key politicians to lead the transitional and conflictual international system towards a cooperative one. While structural and material factors have an impact on the development of events, the "social construction" of the reality through debates, speeches and finally diplomacy plays perhaps the most decisive role. A "new thinking" of Gorbachev certainly created important conditions for the ending of the Cold War. The question is whether the collec-tive identity is overcoming the egoistic identity in the system. Wendt states that

> Even if not intended as such, in other words, the process by which ego-
> ists learn to cooperate is at the same time a process of reconstructing
> their interests in terms of shared commitments to social norms. Over
> time, this will tend to transform a positive interdependence of outcomes
> into a positive interdependence of utilities or collective interest organized
> around the norms of in question.[5]

Russia is undergoing a historical process of transition from tyranny to democracy. The western countries seem, in modern parlance, "clue-less" when trying to cope with this transition. Should they "contain"

Russia by expanding NATO or should Russia be permitted to be entirely incorporated into the Western institutions? A "constructivist" analysis of this problem would suggest that four decades of cooperation may have transformed a positive interdependence of outcomes into a collective "European identity" in terms of which states increasingly define their "self-interest."[6] Containment should not be implemented until Russia actually poses a strategic threat to the rest of the world.[7] Consequently, for the West--the German-driven European Union, that part of the Pacific that is oriented toward the United States, and finally the United States itself and the rest of North America--the strategic choice should be cooperation, not containment, vis-a-vis Russia, the Islamic coalition or China in the foreseeable future.

When economic-political blocs interact in today's multipolar world, much more is going on than realists have traditionally argued. Although international politics

> ...is in part about acting on material incentives in given anarchic worlds, it is also about the reproduction and transformation--by intersubjective dynamics at both the domestic and systemic levels--of the identities and interests through which those incentives and worlds are created.[8]

The integration theorists have been suggesting this for decades. It seems that more emphasis should be given to the argument that fundamental structures of international politics are increasingly social, rather than strictly material, as realists argue; and that these social structures shape actor's identities and interests, rather than just their behavior, as rationalists argue.[9] Although the multipolar system would be replaced with a new bipolarity basically between China and the Euro-Atlantic bloc, it could be, however, an interactive system, and thus, a co-operative one instead of a new Cold War.

Can the international community avoid a "militarization" of security during the years of "fragile multipolarity?" These are the alternatives:

1. the emergence of a new bipolar system and the remilitarization of security;
2. the emergence of global economic and democratic space and the demilitarization of security; or

3. the continuation of "fragile multipolarity" and the de facto remilitarization of security.

I am convinced that the international community still has an opportunity to make a choice for the second alternative, although the trends discussed in this volume indicate that the first may be just as likely. If so, then history would repeat itself. Yet the end of the Cold War was an indication that a major "difference" had been made in the course of mankind's history--a geopolitical shift made without the "help" of hegemonic war.

Kant's vision may have come closer. Empirical studies have indicated that democracies are less likely to fight each other. Jack S. Levy has noted that "this absence of war between democratic states comes as close as anything we have to an empirical law in international relations."[10]

It is important, however, to realize that modernity does not solve the dilemma of war and conflict as such. Democracies are more "peaceful" when in an environment of other democracies. But, unless a secure environment is present (through fortuitous geography or through "free riding" in an alliance), there seems to be less historical evidence for the emergence of long-term stable democracies. In the foreseeable future, capacities are still needed to balance threats and guarantee security; if security is not present, then democracy cannot be nurtured. At the very least, we need to consider whether or not democracy is "security-dependent." If so, then we need to find ways to balance threats and capacities in new ways--by abating threats that confront nascent democracies.[11]

There has never exited a permanently stable order inside the democratic community of nations, either. On the one hand, the racial riots in Los Angeles in 1992, inside the Euro-Atlantic community, indicate that the democratic society tolerates a good deal of internal insecurity. On the other hand, some of the attributes of sociopolitical modernity can also advance without coalescing into a democratic polity. This was especially true in the early days of Mikhail Gorbachev in the former Soviet Union.

It is crucial to note, however, that the relationship among security, democracy and the free market constitutes a basis for a more peace-prone international development in the long run. If so, the political core of this development can be the further evolution of the Euro-Atlantic community, a "zone of civility" in international relations.[12]

This community has to be able to take and maintain the leadership position in the emerging international system, or else the inherent rivalries will keep the system internally fragile. If so, then the community--and the system, for that matter--will be unable to meet the challenges of the 21st century, and global rivalry will ensue.

From Trends to New Realities in 2010

"As a result of these changes, communities and entire countries appear to have less and less control of their own destinies...What is clear is that as the Cold War fades away, we face not a "new world order" but a troubled and fractured planet whose problems deserve the serious attention of politicians and publics alike."

--Paul Kennedy

The United States would center its foreign policy on the countries that determine the overall character of the international system--China, Japan, Russia, members of the European Union, and some of the emerging powers, such as India and Indonesia."

--Charles William Maynes

"The drive of big companies to win world markets and maximize sales overwhelms all but the most draconian protectionism."

--Robert J. Samuelson[13]

The Persian Gulf crisis and the war in Bosnia marked the onset of a new world "security disorder" in the early 1990s. Meanwhile, Asia's rise marked another onset of a new world "economic disorder" in the late 1990s. The old geopolitical world map based on bipolarity has been transferred to the one based on multipolarity. Yet in this multipolar order the United States will remain primus inter pares for years to come. Every multipolar system known in history has collapsed, as one or more of the major powers expressed dissatisfaction with the existing hierarchy, rejected the rules on which they had agreed to manage their relations, and attempted by force to overturn the status quo.

"Rivalry has routinely resulted in a hegemonic struggle for supremacy ending in a new catastrophic general war, each more destructive than the previous one," as two prominent observers reason.[14] The question remaining, then, is (a) whether the emerging multipolar order constitutes a step toward a new hegemonic war, or (b) the cycle of hegemonic wars is finally over.

I have discussed in this volume the economic foundations of the emerging multipolar order. I assume that the trading blocs will constitute the new power centers and that national destinies will be primarily determined by commercial competition, not military conquest. The issues of geoeconomics (the distribution of wealth) have become gradually more important than conventional issues of geopolitics (the distribution of political and military forces). However, the current situation is very complex. Russia as an economic entity has fallen to secondary status but remains a great power militarily and politically. Germany and China are economic giants but are politically and militarily minor players, at least in their own right. I assume, however, that they will assume political and, particularly in the case of China, great power military status through geoeconomics and, in practical terms, through emerging regional trading blocs. I concur with Robert Gilpin, who insists that, while economic forces are important, in the end, "they always work in the context of the political struggle among groups and nations."[15] Political struggle is the subject of Gilpin's *War and Change in World Politics*.[16] I have also interpreted strategic trade theory to suggest that "bitter economic rivalry" is a likely outcome of a new political economy because of fear that "there can be enduring national winners and losers from trade competition." The result would be mercantile rivalry among the world's principal trading blocs in which "fear of one another" may be the only force binding them together.[17] Finally, there is no real room for prosperity and development outside the regional trading blocs.

The most dramatic international system change is related to the changing sizes of the emerging regional trading blocs described in this volume. As demonstrated numerically in the tables in the annex, China *could* become the number one power in the world economy in 2010, the enlarged European Union would be second, the United States third, followed by, at a much lower level, Japan fourth and India fifth. Russia would be out of this competition altogether, lying among a number of other middle-sized economic entities and roughly comparable with Indonesia.[18]

As a strategic result of this change concerning economic development, China must be viewed in connection with Japan and the East Asian tigers and would-be tigers (Singapore, Malaysia, Indonesia, Vietnam). In this context, Asia would constitute the real economic and perhaps political power center of the world, as I have indicated throughout this book. This kind of fundamental change would restructure the international system in strategic terms accordingly. Most obviously, a new bipolarity would loom on the horizon in the early 21st century.

Additionally, future development of the changing international system will be dependent on two issues:

1. obvious protectionism and "trade wars", and their impact on the system (increasing instability and rivalry between the actors); and
2. power-political relations between China and the United States, or perhaps between China on the one hand and the US and the European Union one the other (the possibility of new bipolarity).

In the 1990s, it has become evident that Russia and China have had great difficulty in their respective entries (in the case of the former, perhaps it is fairer to say re-entry) on the world scene, in particular in the global economy. Even taking into account the successes the Chinese have enjoyed, one can speak about mismanagement of their policies. Although no clear single trend has been obvious in the 1990s making trade wars an inevitability between the emerging trading blocs, such conflict is not impossible to envision at the end of the decade or beyond. We can identify in the lexicon and literature of international relations two forms of mercantilism (by which I mean the attempt of governments or "unions" of governments to manipulate economic arrangements in order to maximize their own interests, whether or not this is at the expense of others): "benign" and "malign." Both suggest that economic regionalism is re-establishing itself, but thereafter they differ markedly.

Benign mercantilism entails a degree of protectionism that safe-guards a society's values and interests; it enables said society to retain domestic autonomy and possess valued industries in a world character-ized by the internationalisation of production, global integration of fi-nancial markets, and the diminution of national control. Malevolent mercantilism, on the other hand, refers to the economic clashes of na-tions that was characteristic of the 1930s; its purpose is to triumph over other states. The first strain is defensive; the second is, to repeat our paraphrase of Clausewitz, the conduct of interstate warfare by eco-nomic means.[19]

In the post-Cold War global economy, the first alternative seems to be both valid and obvious. However, a kind of mixed system of mer-cantilistic competition--economic regionalism, at first soft, but later on hard, accompanied by sectoral protectionism--may become the end re-sult. This kind of complex international system, which cannot be fully controlled by the emerging institutions like the WTO, contains many flaws that could engender clashes among protectionistic trading blocs.

I have tried to argue in this book that the old nation-states are now "inside" the emerging trading blocs. Consequently, they still constitute additional causes for social conflict in the future, although now possib-ly through the "cover" of the groupings in which they are now sub-sumed. However, none of these trading blocs--not even the European Union--will be translated into new nation-states; rather they will be-come new types of international entities. Military conflicts between the new entities might possibly be avoided if all of these entities de-velop as, or retain their status, as democratic societies. In 1900, we had barely 25 democracies, a century later more than 100. As noted earlier, Jack S. Levy has recorded that "the absence of war between democratic states comes as close as anything we have to an empirical law in international relations."[20] It is to be hoped that democratically-oriented blocs will be as successful in avoiding war as the democratic states that will comprise many of them.

Unfortunately, China has to face the fact that it will be a subject of fears and misperceptions as it rise to the top rank of global economic powers. Karen Elliott House notes that

...only a few years after the collapse of the Soviet Union, the US once again is faced with a self-defined rival to its sole superpower status. Thus, for all the fashionable talk of multipolarity, the US faces a new bipolar relationship not unlike that between the US and the Soviet Union after World War II.[21]

Consequently, this problematic relationship should be managed with the same kind of consistency that the previous American presidents paid to US-Soviet relations. Furthermore, the new world powers, like the European Union, should be more assertive in their policies. The European Union has its problems in becoming a strong international player. If one wants to have a role in international trade relations, it cannot be done without a strengthened role in political and strategic relations.

One of the problems in managing relations with China results from the fact that it is not a friend, but not a foe either, to the US or to the European Union.

There is nothing in China's recent history that threatens America enough to engage in a costly containment strategy against China. However, China is destined to become a superpower, and at the same time, Russia is doomed to lose the same status. In the past a hegemonic war has resulted from this kind of fundamental strategic shift in power relations. However, a major war can be avoided.[22]

Much is at stake and will depend on the skills and visions of the leaders of the three key actors: China, the European Union and the United States. Russia's role is to join one of them; if isolated, it is too weak to challenge the change anyway. The United States and the European Union have to help China to choose the right road.

Notes

1. Kegley and Wittkopf, *World Politics*, pp. 105-106; Jonathan Clarke, "Rhetoric Before Reality," *Foreign Affairs*, September/October 1995, p. 7.

2. Robert Jervis, *Perception and Misperception in International Politics* (Princeton: Princeton University Press), 1976, pp. 405-406.

3. Coral Bell, Why Russia Should Join NATO," *The National Interest,* Winter 1991, p. 38.

4. Eisuke Sakakibara, "The End of Progressivism--A Search for New Goals," *Foreign Affairs,* September/October 1995, pp. 8-14.

5. Wendt, "Anarchy is What States Make of It," pp. 391-426. Wendt goes on to say that a constructivist analysis of cooperation concentrates "...on how the expectations produced by behavior affect identities and interests. The process of creating institutions is one of internalizing new understandings of self and other, of acquiring new role identities, not just of creating external constraints on the behavior of exogenously constituted actors."

6. On "European identity," see Barry Buzan, et al, (eds.), *The European Security Order Recast* (London: Pinter Publishers), 1990. I am particularly grateful to Henrikka Heikka and Christer Pursiainen, who drew my attention to constructivism as a fruitful tool for analyzing today's international system.

7. See Charles H. Fairbanks, Jr., "A Tired Anarchy," *The National Interest,* Spring 1995, pp. 15-25. Fairbanks makes an excellent argument that "if Russia and her neighbors seem fated for a period of anarchy, it will be a tired anarchy; Russian nationalism is combative, not imperial."

8. Wendt, "Collective Identity Formation and the International State," pp. 386-394.

9. See *International Security,* Summer 1993, pp. 39-93, which contains articles by Robert O. Keohoane and Lisa L. Martin, "The Promise of Institutionalist Theory"; Charles A. Kupchan and Clifford A. Kupchan, "The Promise of Collective Security"; John Gerard Ruggie, "The False Promise of Realism"; Alexander Wendt, "Constructing International Politics"; and John. J. Mearsheimer, "A Realist Reply". These scholars discuss the basic nature of the present world system either on realist, rationalist or constructivist premises.

10. Jack S. Levy, "The Causes of War: A Review of Theories and Evidence," in Philip E. Tetlock, et al (eds.), *Behavior, Society and Nuclear War* (New York: Oxford University Press).

11. David A. Lake, "Powerful Pacifists: Democratic States and War,"*American Political Science Review,* March 1992, pp. 24-37.

12. Kalevi J. Holsti, "A 'Zone of Civility' in European Diplomatic Relations? The CSCE and Conflict Resolution," (Paper presented at the annual meeting of the International Studies Association, Atlanta, GA, March/April 1992).

13. Kennedy, *Preparing for the Twenty-First Century,* pp. 333, 349; Charles William Maynes, "Bottom-Up Foreign Policy," *Foreign Policy,* Autumn 1996, pp. 35-53; quoted in Benjamin Barber, *Jihad vs. McWorld* (New York: Ballantine Books), 1995, p. 28.

14. Kegley and Wittkopf, *World Politics,* p. 95.

15. Robert G. Gilpin, "The Richness of the Tradition of Political Realism," in Robert Keohane (ed.), *Neorealism and its Critics* (New York: Columbia University Press), 1986, p. 310.

16. Robert G. Gilpin, *War and Change in World Politics* (Cambridge: Cambridge University Press), 1981.

17. Michael Borrus, Steve Weber, and Joseph Willinganz, "Mercantilism and Global Security," *The National Interest*, Volume 29, Fall 1992, pp. 21-29.

18. In 1993 dollars, the GDP figures were the following: US--$6.4 trillion; the EU--$6.1 trillion; and Japan--$3.9 trillion. In comparison, Russia was in 11th place--$350 billion. See Dr. Pekka Visuri's forthcoming book, *Turvallisuuspolitiikan Strategia (Strategy of Security Policy)* (Helsinki: WSOY), 1997.

19. Gilpin, *The Political Economy of International Relations*, p. 404. In the mid-1990s, China and Russia wanted to join the WTO but they were told by member- states that they must first open their economies and even parts of their political and social systems. See also Barry Buzan and Gerald Segal, "The Rise of 'Lite' Powers," *World Policy Journal*, Fall 1996, pp. 1-10.

20. Levy, "The Causes of War."

21. Karen Elliott House, Who Will Manage the Next Superpower?" *The Wall Street Journal*, November 26, 1996.

22. Ibid.

Appendix

Asia Arms as the World Cuts Back:
Post-Cold War Changes in Defense Budgets (1990-95)

	1990	1991	1992	1993	1994	1995	% change
US	291.4	3.0	270.9	258.9	251.4	252.6	-13.3
USSR	116.7	--	--	--	--	--	--
Russia	--	--	85.9	75.1	78.5	62.8	-26.9[a]
Japan	28.7	32.7	35.9	39.7	42.1	53.8	+87.5
PRC	6.1	6.1	6.7	7.3	6.7	7.5	+23.0[b]
Taiwan	8.7	9.3	10.3[c]	10.5	11.3	NA	+29.9[c]
S. Korea	10.6	10.8	11.2	12.1	14.0	14.4	+35.8
North Korea[d]	5.3	2.4	2.1	2.2	2.3	2.2	-58.5
Viet Nam[d]	NA	1.9	1.8	NA	0.9	0.9	NA
Indo-nesia	1.5	1.6	1.8	2.0	2.3	2.6	+73.3
Aus-tralia	7.0	7.1	7.0	7.0	6.9	7.4	-5.7

Source: International Institute for Strategic Studies, *The Military Balance* (1990-96 editions)
(*note: Figures in billions of US dollars unless otherwise indicated. Figures are for defense budgets, which indicate intended level of effort and for which more recent data are available, rather than defense expenditures. Data do not correct for exchange rate fluctuations and hence exaggerate some claims.*)

[a] 1992-94
[b] IISS estimated actual Chinese expenditures are much higher: $18.1 billion for 1991, $24.3 billion for 1992, $27.4 billion for 1993, and $28.5 billion for 1994.
[c] 1990-94
[d] estimates

Emerging Asian Oil Import Rivalry

Importing Nation	Share of Total Asian Oil Imports (%)		
	1992	**2000**	**2010**
Japan	77.4	43.2	36.5
China	--	10.9	19.4
Taiwan/Hong Kong	10.0	9.7	9.0
South Korea	21.0	20.3	18.3
ASEAN	--	5.9	16.9

Source: APEC International Advisory Committee for Energy Intermediate Report (June 1, 1995)
(notes: Based on 1995 national energy supply-demand projection in metric tons of oil equivalent (MTOE) for Japan, China, Taiwan/Hong Kong, South Korea and ASEAN; 8.4% of net 1992 imports into the nations listed were from China and ASEAN.)

Prospective Key Players in the Emerging Asian Power Game

Country	GNP	Pop. (MM)	Defense Budget	Armed Forces	Nuclear Capacity
Japan	$4.592 tn	125	$53.8 bn	239,500	near nuclear
China	$509 bn	1,201	$7.5 bn	2,930,000	yes
Korea (N and S)	$401 bn	69	$16.6 bn	1,761,000	residual capacity
Russia	$1.120 tn	149	$62.8 bn	1,520,000	yes
India	$270 bn	934	$8.1 bn	1,145,000	undeclared
Vietnam	$19 bn	74	$900 mn	572,000	no
US	$6.737 tn	263	$252.6 bn	1,547,000	undeclared

Source: International Institute for Strategic Studies, *The Military Balance* (1995-96 editions) (notes: *All figures for 1994, except defense budgets, which are for fiscal 1995. Actual Chinese expenditures are believed to be much higher than the nominal defense budget, mainly because of the use of profits by defense enterprises for military purposes. Estimates for 1995 defense budget, for example, range between $7.5 billion-$50 billion. See Far Eastern Economic Review, April 13, 1995, p. 25.*)

GDP (in US$ billions) of Six Potential Trading Blocs (based on Purchasing Power Parity–PPP)

	1996	1997	1998	1999	2000	2001	2002
European Union[a]	7088.9	7265.9	7451.9	7643.1	7821.3	8000	8187.1
United States[b]	7097.6	72673.9	7408.7	7567.5	7735.3	7903.5	8068.2
Japan	2777.2	2842.6	2931.8	2999.5	3062.7	3134.7	3220.6
Russia[c]		651	670.3	690.4	711.1	732.4	754.4
China[d]	3669.1	3999.3	4359.2	4751.4	5449.2	5857.9	6297.2
India	1257.4	1296.4	1336.5	1504.6	1551	1609	1668

	2003	2004	2005	2006	2007	2008	2009	2010
European Union[a]	8380	8578.8	8782.5	8991.6	9204.8	9421.7	9642.2	9866.7
United States[b]	8228.8	8388.9	8554.1	8730.2	8914.6	9102.9	9292.5	9481.9
Japan	3319.1	3426.1	3539.1	3657.5	3781.9	3909.6	4037.9	4165.8
Russia[c]	777	800.3	824.3	849	874.5	900.7	927.7	955.5
China[d]	6769.5	7277.2	7823.1	8409.8	9040.6	10501.6	11289.2	12135.8
India	1730	2087	2164	2244	2327	2413	2502	2595

Source: Finnish Institute of International Affairs

[a] Enlarged EU   [b] NAFTA   [c] CIS   [d] Chinese economic area

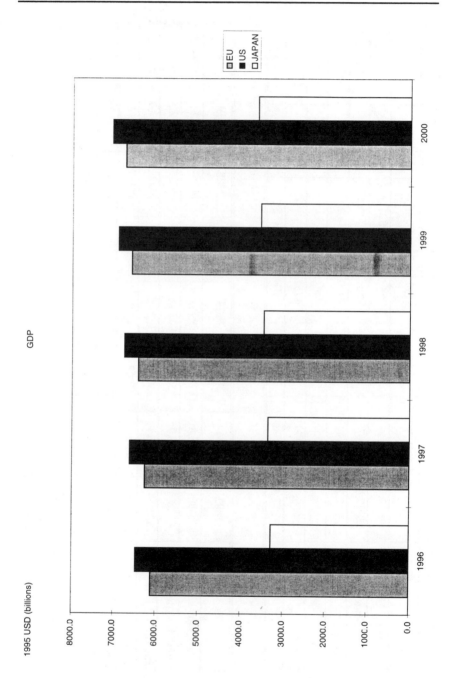

GDP

1995 USD (billions)

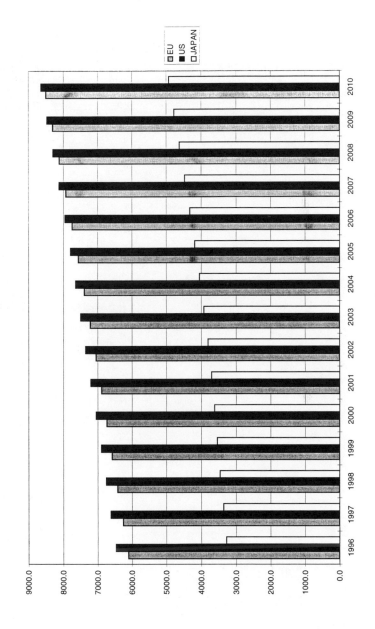

GDP IN KEY TRADING AREAS

1990 USD (billions)

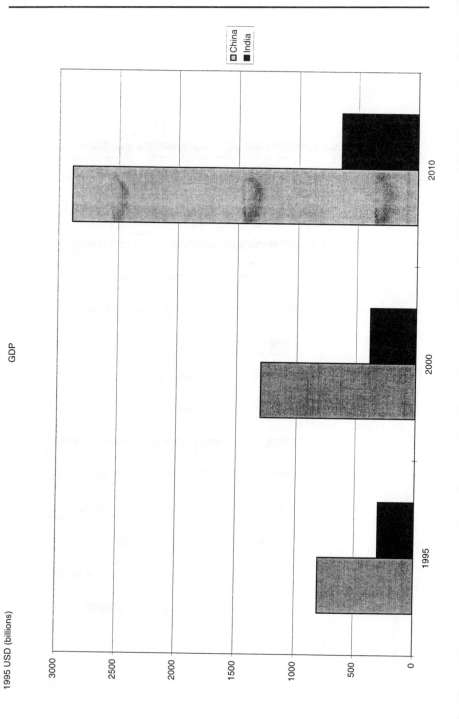

GDP

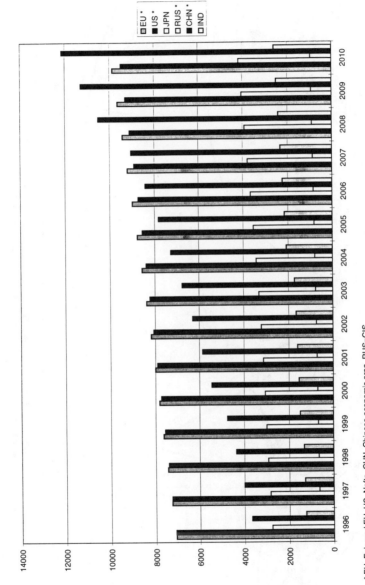

PPP GDP IN 1995 USD**

WORLD ECONOMY PPP GDP ON KEY TRADING AREAS

* EU=Enlarged EU, US=Nafta, CHN=Chinese economic area, RUS=CIS
** CHN and IND in 1994 USD

By Riku Warjovaara
The Finnish Institute of International Affiars

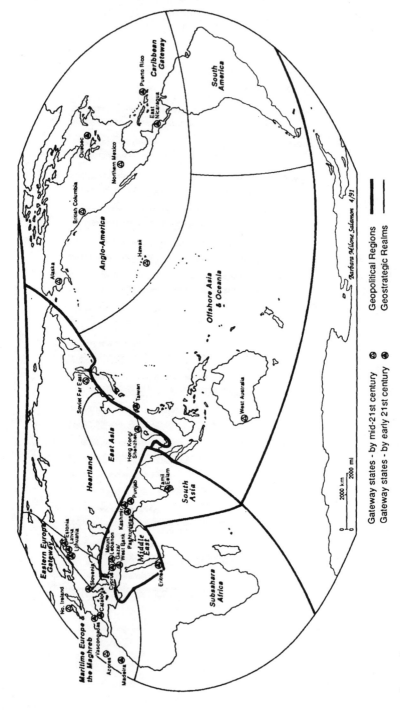

Prospective gateway states. SOURCE: Saul B. Cohen, "Geopolitical Change in the Post–Cold War Era," *Annals of the Association of American Geographers*, vol. 81, no. 4 (December 1991).

Address by Secretary of State Warren Christopher
On U.S. National Interest in the Asia-Pacific Region

National Press Club   Washington, D.C.
July 28, 1995

...tomorrow I depart on my sixth trip to Asia as Secretary of State. First, I go to Brunei for the annual meeting of the ASEAN group--the Association of Southeast Asian Nations. Then I go to Malaysia to meet with that country to try to strengthen our ties with a country of increasing importance. Then to Cambodia, whereas Bud says I'll be the first Secretary of State to visit since John Foster Dulles, and have a chance to reaffirm our support for the efforts of the people of that country to overcome what is a very tragic past. And then to Vietnam, which is a trip that I greatly look forward to, to have an opportunity to carry forward the normalization that President Clinton announced in a very farsighted way the other day, and also to continue to pursue the high priority that the President has given to getting the fullest possible accounting of information with respect to the POWs and MIAs.

Over the past half century, I have personally witnessed many of the historic changes that have swept the Pacific. As a teenager, I moved to Los Angeles and watched California build links between the Far West and the Far East. As a young ensign in the U.S. Navy in World War II, I saw the Asia-Pacific region devastated by four years of war. As a young negotiator in the textile talks in Japan in the early 1960s, I saw firsthand the region poised for a very rapid economic growth. And now as a still- young--well, almost--Secretary of State, I see a region with extraordinary potential for prosperity, stability, and democracy.

This hopeful turn of events would not have come to pass without the indispensable role played by the United States. After World War II, America's leaders understood that a secure and prosperous Asia was vital to our national interest. Our military presence promoted stability. It gave nations in the region a chance to build thriving economies for the benefit of all.

The transformation of the Asia-Pacific region that has taken place since World War II is truly breathtaking. In the space of half a century, nations that were among the oldest outposts of colonialism are now among the newest frontiers and most successful exponents of capitalism. Underdeveloped, largely rural societies have moved to dynamic modern economies offering broad opportunities to all the peoples of their countries.

These economic miracles are increasingly associated with the spread of political freedoms and vibrant social societies. As a result, we are turning the seas and skies that once divided us into channels of communication and cooperation.

The trade and investment dollars that stream between Asia and America create jobs and propel our economic growth. Our nation, I should emphasize also, has been enriched by millions of Asian Americans imbued with the values of education and hard work and family--values that are just as important to Americans as they are to Asians--and with it a stream of marvelous Asian students in our universities, probably the most numerically largest, and in many ways the most successful, of our foreign students in our universities.

On the fiftieth anniversary of the end of the Second World War, American leadership in Asia remains as essential to our security and prosperity as ever before. With the end of the Cold War, the political landscape in Asia is undergoing really profound changes. Nowhere is this more apparent than in the largest powers in Asia -- Russia, China, and Japan. So in this time of great uncertainty and change, a stable U.S. presence seems to me to be increasingly important, and that is why President Clinton has renewed and reinforced our commitment to be and remain a Pacific power.

Our strategy in the region recognizes the new opportunities and challenges that are posed by the post-Cold War world. Fortunately, this region is now remarkably free of conflict. But while no major power views another power as an immediate military threat, there is a considerable danger that age-old rivalries could be rekindled.

There is also the problem that the dynamic economic growth that is spurring integration is at the same time creating new tensions, as there is a competition for resources and markets. With the growth of those markets and those economies and with new technologies have also come the spread of weapons of mass destruction. There has also come the emergence of very ugly networks of narcotics suppliers as well as very severe pressures on the environment from the growing econo-mies.

No single nation in the Pacific can confront these complex chal-lenges all on its own. Certainly they can best be met through a com-munity of nations acting together--a very diverse community, to be sure, but one that's increasingly linked by shared values as well as shared interests.

The leadership of the United States will be essential to bringing that community of the Pacific to life. To ensure a peaceful and prosperous Asia-Pacific for the 21st Century, we've adopted what I describe as a four-part strategy.

First, we will maintain and invigorate our core alliances with Japan, Korea, Australia, the Philippines, and Thailand.

Second, we're actively pursuing a policy of engagement with the other leading countries in the region, including--and, perhaps, especial-ly including--our former Cold War adversaries.

Third, we're building a regional architecture that will sustain eco-nomic growth, promote integration, and assure stability over the longer term.

And, fourth, we're supporting democracy and human rights, which serves our ideals as well as our interests.

Let me tell you a little bit about each of those four points.

Our strategy begins with our core alliances because we understand that security must come first. Our military presence remains the foun-dation for stability and prosperity in a region where the interests of four majorpowers intersect. This military presence is our first line of defense. It safeguards our allies. It protects our economic interest. And it reassures a region that is still troubled by historical antago-nisms. That's why our security presence in the Asia-Pacific region is so broadly welcomed. I've really been struck over and over again by how often countries in the region are anxious to hear us say that we're going to remain a Pacific power, and we'll remain in the region.

Our administration's bottom-up review of U.S. defense policy at the beginning of our Administration confirmed the continuing need for a forward-deployed presence in Asia, and hence the United States is committed to maintaining approximately 100,000 troops in the Paci-fic--the equivalent of how many we plan to maintain in Europe.

American policy toward Asia begins with Japan. The United States-Japan partnership is the very cornerstone of our engagement in the Asia-Pacific region. Fifty years ago, the United States made a strategic choice to help Japan rebuild. Today our democratic, our alliance with the democratic and prosperous Japan is one of the real successes of the post-war era.

Our challenge now is to assure that the next five decades with Japan are as effective and prosperous as the last five decades have been.

I'm struck by how few Americans know that we are maintaining 47,000 U.S. troops in Japan, and that's in addition to the men and women in the Seventh Fleet. Their presence is no Cold War anachronism, as soon commentators have recently claimed. On the contrary, these American troops, which are stationed in Japan, are a very wise investment in the future security of the region. They provide a stabilizing presence for all the nations of Asia.

Last November, the United States and Japan launched a new dialogue to renew and enhance our security ties. I'm pleased to have been part of that, as the Defense and Foreign Ministers of our two countries are examining very important issues like the interoperability of our forces which, of course, are enhanced when Japan purchases our U.S. weapons systems which, fortunately, they so often do.

This new dialogue is also concentrating on such things as host nation support under which Japan provides 70 percent of the cost of our presence in Japan, another fact that is really not very well known to the American people. And we are deepening our global cooperation which has been very valuable, as Japan has begun to participate in peacekeeping endeavors in such places as Cambodia and Mozambique and Rwanda.

In the post-Cold War world, we feel that Japan is in a position to take on even greater responsibilities than in the past, and that is why we are supporting Japan's bid to become a permanent member of the U.N. Security Council.

Together we are doing a number of important things already. For example, supporting reform in Russia, peace in the Middle East, and stability in Haiti. And together we are addressing complex global issues like unsustainable population growth, AIDs and pollution through what we call our common agenda. And so, working together, what we have done together, makes us feel that Japan can even do more to take its place as one of the great countries in the world.

As the two largest economies in the world, America and Japan also share a responsibility to uphold the goal of open trade and to support the international financial system. Our administration has consistently sought to open Japan's markets, a role that we have taken because we know it will benefit American businesses and American workers, as well as Japanese consumers and the rest of the world.

Under the U.S.-Japan economic framework, we have reached 16 new agreements that expand our access and the access of the rest of the world to Japan's markets--16 agreements just since we have been in office in the last two-and-a-half years.

Last month, as you know, we concluded an important agreement with Japan that will widen the access to Japan's markets for autos and auto parts, and last week we resolved a dispute over air cargo.

While each of these 16 and, I guess, now 18 agreements are important in themselves, we also need to work to implement the agreements, so they aren't just agreements on a shelf but are implemented in the market place, and that will be crucial for the United States.

Our relationship with Japan is a multifaceted partnership. It will achieve its broadest potential when all of the elements are strong--strategic and military, diplomatic and political, and economic, as well.

Let me turn now to Korea. It is really a great tribute to the Republic of Korea that our longstanding military and security alliance has now become a mature and important complete partnership. Yesterday President Clinton and President Kim Young Sam of Korea unveiled a Korean war memorial that pays tribute somewhat belatedly to the shared sacrifice that sealed our alliance more than 40 years ago.

Now that South Korea is a vibrant democracy, as well as a valued trading partner and a trusted comrade-in-arms, our relationship is stronger than ever before.

The U.S. security commitment to South Korea, which is demonstrated by the 37,000 American troops who are stationed there, a somewhat better-known statistic, that security relationship and our commitment to them remains unshakable. Over the last two years, our determined diplomacy has put the North Korean nuclear issue on the road to resolution.

The agreed framework between the United States and North Korea has frozen North Korea's nuclear program. When this is fully implemented, the framework will eliminate entirely their dangerous nuclear program.

As North Korea carries out its obligations under the framework, it can begin to develop more normal relationships with United States and the other nations of the region.

But I'd have to say that any major improvement in our relationships with the North can come only with progress in relationships between the two Koreas.

In this context, recent talks between the North and the South on supplying much-needed rice to Pyongyang are a really quite hopeful development. The resumption of a broader dialogue between North and South, especially a dialogue on the issue of a nuclear-free peninsula offers the only really meaningful hope for reduced tensions and ultimate reconciliation on the peninsula.

The second element of our Pacific strategic is our policy of engagement with the other leading powers of the region, and, as I said, including especially our former Cold War adversaries.

In that connection, of course, few nations are able to play as large a role in shaping Asia's future as is China. With its vast population, its geographic reach, its rich history of cultural influence across Asia, its growing military power and its new economic dynamism, China is just unique.

As we shape our policy and as we conduct our diplomacy with China, we must not allow short-term calculation to divert us from pursuing our long-term interests.

I need not tell this sophisticated and experienced audience that we are going through a period of difficulty in this important relationship.

One immediate cause of China's concern is that the recent private visit of Taiwan's leader, Lee Teng-hui, to his alma mater of Cornell, represents a shift in our approach to China.

Let me say that this concern is unwarranted. The private visit by Lee Teng-hui was a special situation, and a courtesy consistent with

American values and opinion. It did not constitute a shift in our policy toward China and Taiwan.

The United States has not and does not intend to change its long-standing one China policy. In this moment of difficulty, it's more important than ever for China, Taiwan and the United States to focus and reflect on the shared interest we have in maintaining the continuity of this policy.

It is a policy that especially and emphatically is in the interests of all of us together.

Over 20 years ago, the United States and China made the strategic choice to end more than two decades of confrontation. Since then, six American Presidents, both Democrats and Republicans alike, have pursued a policy of engagement with China that has served and is serving the enduring interests of everybody, United States and all the others in the region.

The policy of engagement reflects the fundamental understanding that our ability to pursue significant common interests and to manage significant disinterests, would not be served by any attempt to isolate or contain China. We do not intend to try to do so.

The wisdom of this historic judgment of engagement has demonstrated time and again that our ability to work together on key challenges of regional and global importance will be best manifested by being engaged; by working together on such issues as the North Korean nuclear issue where China was of some help; and on the extension of the Non-Proliferation Treaty where we worked together at the United Nations.

The virtues of this policy of engagement have also been demonstrated by the benefits of our success together in Cambodia, as well as the launching of the new regional security dialogues under the ASEAN umbrella.

Since 1972, the basis for our engagement has been our one China policy. We have consistently followed the basic principles developed in the Shanghai Communique of 1972, the 1979 Communique establishing diplomatic relations, and the 1982 U.S.-China Communique on arms sales.

Pursuant to these vital documents, we recognize that the Government of the PRC is the sole legal government of China. We acknowledge the Chinese position that there is but one China, and that Taiwan is part of China. We reaffirm that we have no intention of advocating or supporting a policy of two Chinas or one China/one Taiwan.

This policy has produced enormous benefits for the United States as well as for China and Taiwan. It has helped to keep the peace, and it has helped to fuel prosperity on both sides of the Strait, and it is certainly helping to propel Taiwan's flourishing democracy.

Just as we look to the continued strengthening of the U.S.-China relationship, we also expect that the unofficial ties between the American people and the people of Taiwan, pursuant to the Taiwan Relations Act of 1979, that those ties will also thrive.

The United States, China and Taiwan share a strong responsibility to pursue policies that foster continued stability in the region. Managing our differences with China on Taiwan and other issues does not mean downplaying their importance. For example, on human rights we still have profound disagreements. We will continue to promote universally recognized human rights in China as well as elsewhere.

We also have serious concerns with respect to the proliferation of weapons of mass destruction. Today such weapons and their delivery pose the greatest threat to global security. As a nuclear power, China, just as the United States does, has special responsibilities. Since the outset of our administration, we've made the case to China that curbing proliferation of weapons of mass destruction is in the overriding mutual interest of all of us.

We are concerned particularly about arms transfers to volatile regions like South Asia and to rogue regimes like Iran. The best way we feel to resolve these concerns is through dialogue between the United States and China, and that is why I urge China to resume our discussions on non- proliferation matters.

Just as we have a mutual interest in holding the spread of weapons of mass destruction, we also share with China an interest in assuring regional stability. As China seeks to modernize its military forces, greater transparency about its military capabilities and its military intentions could do a great deal to reassure its neighbors. Our differences with China are an argument for engagement, not for containment or isolation. Neither the United States nor China can afford the luxury of walking away from our responsibility to manage our differences.

China has as much interest in maintaining constructive relationships as we do.

Let me say that China can take an immediate step to help restore a more positive atmosphere with the immediate release of American citizen Harry Wu.

Moving on to another subject and area, I look forward to meeting with Foreign Minister Qian Qichen of China in Brunei when I go there this weekend. I'll be meeting with him on August 1. I intend to discuss with him at that time the fundamentals of our relationship, to reiterate the continuity of our policy, to address candidly our areas of agreement and disagreement, and to seek to restore the positive momentum in our relationship that marked the earlier period. A strong, stable, open and prosperous China can be a valuable partner for the United States and a responsible leader of the international community.

A week from tomorrow I will arrive in Hanoi. Since taking office, President Clinton has made his top priority with respect to Vietnam the fullest possible accounting of our prisoners of war and those missing in action. We have been encouraged by the results of Hanoi's recent cooperation during the months we've been in office.

We're convinced that normalizing relations is the best way to keep up this momentum and to achieve further results. That is why after a decade of war and two decades of estrangement the President made his courageous decision to establish diplomatic relations between our two countries. Let me add that I have been personally inspired by the opportunity to work with the elected leaders of both parties, including Senator John McCain and Senator John Kerry and Senator Bob Kerrey and Representative Pete Peterson to bring about this normalization and to help close a very bitter chapter in our nation's history.

Closer engagement with Vietnam is in America's interest in many ways, in addition to the POW and MIA issue. We can work together to promote economic reform, to focus on the rule of law, human rights, regional peace and stability, and to pursue areas of common interest, like the fight against narcotics trafficking.

Similarly, engagement with other leading nations of Asia is crucial to our interest in that burgeoning region. Indonesia, Malaysia and Singapore are dynamic countries from an economic standpoint which can make important contributions to regional stability and thus are very important parts of our dialogue in Asia.

In the long run, however, despite the advantages of these bilateral contacts, we need to build mechanisms of cooperation on a multilateral basis to assure that the current favorable environment will endure. Thus, the third element of our strategy is to build a sound architecture for regional cooperation.

The creation of the ASEAN Regional Forum is an important initial step in this process. This forum reflects what might be called the ASEAN way of doing things: consultation, consensus and coopera-tion. We see this forum and the emerging security dialogue in north-east Asia as crucial supplements to our alliances and to our forward military presence in the Asia- Pacific region.

Next week in Brunei, I'll join my colleagues from 17 Asia-Pacific nations and the European Union for the second meeting of the ASEAN Regional Forum. We'll be discussing security challenges such as the North Korean nuclear issue and the importance of freedom of navigation.

In this connection, let me emphasize that we've consistently urged the claimants to the resources in the Spratly Islands in the South China Sea to resolve their differences through dialogue and not through any military confrontation.

These important but nascent efforts to build mechanisms for security cooperation in Asia complement the remarkable economic integration that the nations are in the process of achieving through APEC. These significant accomplishments are attributable in no small part to Presi-dent Clinton's vision in convening the first ever APEC leaders' meet-ing two years ago in Seattle. Then last year in Bogor in Indonesia, the APEC leaders committed to achieve free trade in the Asia-Pacific re-gion by the year 2020. And this year in the Osaka meeting of APEC in November, leaders will turn this historic vision from the Bogor Conference into a blueprint for action, a blueprint which should set forth the shared principles, specific goals, and a process for achieving them by 2020.

The fourth and final element of our strategy is our steadfast support for human rights and democracy. Just as open markets and open sea lanes promote prosperity and security in the Pacific, so do open societies. Business people in Shanghai and in San Francisco may speak quite different languages, but they agree that enterprise survives and thrives best when ideas and information are freely exchanged. The experiences of many democracies across the region tell us that accountable government and the rule of law are the bedrock of stability and prosperity.

On the other hand, the experiences of countries like Burma and North Korea tell us that repression only entrenches poverty. Open societies do make better neighbors. History shows us that the greatest threats to security in the Asia-Pacific region have come from governments that flout the rule of law at home and reject it abroad.

On human rights issues, every nation must find its own way, consistent with its history and culture. But at the same time, all have a responsibility to meet international obligations and to respect the standards of the Universal Declaration of Human Rights. America will continue to champion human rights in the movement toward open societies and we'll do so without arrogance but also without apologies.

In this connection, we'll continue to assist countries that are embracing democracies--new democracies such as Cambodia and Mongolia--to assist them in the development of their political parties, to try to advise them on the development of their political institutions.

In Burma, the efforts of the United States and the international community have helped to lead to the recent release of the imprisoned opposition leader, distinguished Nobel Prize winner, Aung San Suu Kyi. We welcome this step, but we believe that its true significance will depend ultimately on whether or not it represents a real movement toward the restoration of democratic government.

I might say we're particularly interested in seeing movement toward an accountable government in Burma since it is the world's largest supplier of heroin.

In sum, my trip to the region, starting tomorrow morning, will advance the four key elements of our Asia-Pacific strategy: reaffirmation of our alliances, engagement with Asia's leading powers, construction of an enduring mechanism for regional cooperation, and support for human rights and democracy. Taken together, these elements will advance our broad-ranging interests in a region that is so vital to both our security and prosperity.

Together with our Asian friends, we've traveled an enormous distance since the end of the war in the Pacific half a century ago. American leadership and American engagement have been absolutely essential on that great journey. It will be no less so as we seek to shrink the distances that separate us and to create a promising Pacific future that all of us can profitably and securely share.

Thank you very much.

Bibliography

Books

Axelrod, Robert, *The Evolution of Cooperation* (New York: Basic Books), 1984.

Baranovsky, Vladimir, and Spanger, Hans-Joachim, (eds.), *In From the Cold: Germany, Russia and the Future of Europe* (Boulder, CO: Westview Press), 1993.

Barber, Benjamin R., *Jihad vs. McWorld* (New York: Ballantine Books), 1995.

Burns, Arthur Lee, *Of Powers and Their Politics* (Englewood Cliffs, NJ: Prentice-Hall), 1964.

Buzan, Barry, et al., (eds.), *The European Security Order Recast* (London: Pinter Publishers), 1990.

Calder, Kent E., *Asia's Deadly Triangle: How Arms, Energy and Growth Threaten to Destabilize Asia* (London: Nicholas Publishing), 1996.

Chomsky, Noam, *World Orders Old and New* (London: Pluto Press), 1994.

Cox, Robert W., *Production, Power and World Order: Social Forces in the Making of History* (New York: Columbia University Press), 1987.

Dannreuther, Roland, *The Middle East in Transition* (Oslo: Institut for Forsvarsstudier), 1995.

Fairgrieve, James, *Geography and World Power* (London: University of London Press), 1915.

Fallows, James, *Looking at the Sun: The Rise of the New East Asian Economic and Political System* (New York: Pantheon), 1994.

Gaddis, John Lewis, *The United States and the End of the Cold War* (New York: Oxford University Press), 1992.

Galtung, Johan, *The True Worlds* (New York: Free Press), 1979.

Gilpin, Robert G., *The Political Economy of International Relations* (Princeton: Princeton University Press), 1987.

--------, *War and Change in World Politics* (Cambridge: Cambridge University Press), 1981.

Holsti, Kalevi J., *Peace and War: Armed Conflicts and International Order 1648-1989* (Cambridge: Cambridge University Press), 1991.

Jervis, Robert, *Perception and Misperception in International Politics* (Princeton: Princeton University Press), 1976.

Kaplan, Morton, *System and Process in International Politics* (New York: John Wiley & Sons), 1957.

Kegley, Charles W., Jr. and Raymond, Gregory A., *A Multipolar Peace? Great-Power Politics in the Twenty-first Century* (New York: St. Martin's Press), 1994.

---------, and Wittkopf, Eugene R., *World Politics: Trends and Transformation* (fifth edition) (New York: St. Martin's Press), 1995.

Kennedy, Paul, *Preparing for the Twenty-first Century* (New York: Random House), 1993.

---------, *The Rise and Fall of the Great Powers* (London: Random House Publishers), 1987.

Keohane, Robert O., *After Hegemony: Cooperation and Discord in the World Political Economy* (Princeton: Princeton University Press), 1984.

---------, and Nye, Joseph S., *Power and Interdependence: World Politics in Transition* (Boston: Little, Brown & Co.), 1989

Kissinger, Henry A., *Diplomacy* (New York: Simon & Schuster), 1994.

Koh, Tommy T.B., *The United States and East Asia: Conflict and Cooperation* (Singapore: Institute of Policy Studies), 1995.

Krasner, Stephen D., *International Regimes* (Ithaca, NY: Cornell University Press), 1984.

Korey, William, *The Promises We Keep: Human Rights, the Helsinki Process, and American Foreign Policy* (New York: St. Martin's Press), 1993.

Mandelbaum, Michael, *The Dawn of Peace in Europe* (New York: Twentieth Century Fund), 1996.

--------- (ed.), *Postcommunism: Four Perspectives* (New York: Council on Foreign Relations Press), 1996.

--------- (ed.), *The Strategic Quadrangle in East Asia* (New York: Council on Foreign Relations Press), 1994.

Mesquita, Bruce Bueno, *The War Trap* (New Haven, CT: Yale University Press), 1981.

Miscamble,Wilson, *George F. Kennan and the Making of American Foreign Policy: 1947-1950* (Princeton: Princeton University Press), 1992.

Modelski,George, *Long Cycles in World History* (London: Macmillan), 1987.

Mueller, John, *Retreat from Doomsday: The Obsolescence of Major War* (New York: Basic Books), 1989.

Niebuhr, Reinhold, *Nations and Empires: Recurring Patterns in the Political Order* (London: Faber and Faber), 1960.

Nye, Joseph S., Jr., *Bound to Lead: The Changing Nature of American Power* (New York: Basic Books), 1990.

O'Neill, Michael, *The Politics of European Integration: A Reader* (London and New York: Routledge), 1996.

Oye, Kenneth, *Cooperation Under Anarchy* (Princeton: Princeton University Press), 1985.

Righter, Rosemary, *Utopia Lost: The United Nations and World Order* (New York: Twentieth Century Fund), 1995.

Rosecrance, Richard Rosecrance, *The Rise of the Trading State: Commerce and Conquest in the Modern World* (New York: Basic Books), 1985.

Rusi, Alpo, *After the Cold War: Europe's New Political Architecture*, (London: Macmillan; New York: St. Martin's Press), 1991.

Russet, Bruce, *Grasping the Democratic Peace: Principles for a Post-Cold War World* (Princeton: Princeton University Press), 1993.

Edward Said, *The World, The Text, and the Critic* (London: Vintage), 1971.

Sandholtz, Wayne; Borrus, Michael, et al., *The Highest Stakes: The Economic Foundations of the New Security System* (New York: Oxford University Press), 1992

Schott, Jeffrey J., *The Uruguay Round: An Assessment* (Washington, DC: Institute for International Economics), 1994.

Schwartz, Herman, *States Versus Markets* (New York: St. Martin's Press), 1994.

Singer, Max and Wildavsky, Aaron, *The Real World Order: Zones of Peace, Zones of Turmoil* (London: Chatham House Publishers), 1993.

Spero, Joan Edelman, *The Politics of International Economic Relations* (fourth ed.), (New York: St. Martin's Press), 1990.

Strange, Susan, *States and Markets* (London: Pinter Publishers), 1988.

Taylor, Peter J., *Britain and the Cold War: 1945 as a Geopolitical Transition* (London: Pinter Publishers), 1990.

Thurow, Lester, *Head to Head: The Coming Economic Battle Among Japan, Europe, and America* (New York: Warner Books), 1993.

Visuri, Pekka, *Turvallisuuspolitiikan Strategia (Strategy of Security Policy)* (Helsinki: WSOY), 1997 (forthcoming).

Wallerstein, Immanuel, *The Modern World System: Capitalist Agriculture and the Origins of the European World Economy in the Sixteenth Century* (New York: Academic Press), 1974.

Waltz, Kenneth N., *Theory of International Politics,* (Wesley, MA: Addison Publishers), 1979.

Wolff, Edward N., *Top Heavy: A Study of Increasing Inequality of Wealth in America* (New York: New Press), 1995.

Young, Oran, *International Cooperation: Building Regimes Upon Natural Resources and the Environment* (Ithaca, NY: Cornell University Press), 1989.

Zänker, Alfred, *Epoche der Entscheidungen: Deutschland, Eurasien und die Welt von Morgen,* (Asendorf: MUT-Verlag), 1992.

Articles and Miscellany

Adomeit, Hannes, "Russia as a 'Great Power' in World Affairs: Images and Reality," *International Affairs,* Vol. 71, 1995.

Aho, C. Michael, "America and the Pacific Century: Trade Conflict and Cooperation?" *International Affairs*, Number 1, 1993.

Aliber, Robert Z., "Three Scenarios for the World Economy," *Ethics & International Affairs*, Vol. 2, 1988.

Amaturo, Wilfried L., "Literature and International Relations: The Question of Culture in the Production of International Power," *Millenius,* Number 1, 1995.

Babi, Don, *"General Agreement on Tariffs and Trade,"* in Kriege, Joe, (ed.), *The Oxford Companion to Politics of the World* (New York: Oxford University Press), 1993.

Bell, Coral, "Why Russia Should Join NATO," *The National Interest,* Winter 1991.

Bergsten, C. Fred, "Globalizing World Trade," *Foreign Affairs,* May/June 1996.

Bhagwati, Jagdishi, "Shock Treatments," *The New Republic,* March 28, 1994.

Binyan, Liu, "Civilization Grafting: No Culture is an Island," *Foreign Affairs,* September/October 1993.

Borrus, Michael; Weber, Steve; and Willinganz, Joseph, "Mercantilism and Global Security," *The National Interest,* Volume 29, Fall 1992.

Brzezinski, Zbigniew, "The Premature Partnership," *Foreign Affairs,* March/ April 1994.

Buzan, Barry, and Segal, Gerald, "The Rise of 'Lite' Powers," *World Policy Journal,* Fall 1996.

Cable, Vincent, "Key Trends in the European Economy and Future," in Miall, Hugh, (ed.), *Redefining Europe: New Patterns of Conflict and Cooperation* (London: Pinter Publishers), 1994.

Carlisle, Charles R., "Is the World Ready for Free Trade?" *Foreign Affairs,* Volume 75, Number 6.

Chase, Robert S.; Hill, Emily B.; and Kennedy, Paul, "Pivotal States and US Strategy," *Foreign Affairs,* January/February 1996.

Clarke, Jonathan, "Rhetoric Before Reality," *Foreign Affairs,* September/October 1995.

Cohen, Saul B., *"Geopolitics in the New World Era: A New Perspective on an Old Discipline,"* in Demko, George J., and Wood, William B., (eds.), *Reordering the World: Geopolitical Perspectives on the 21st Century* (Boulder, CO: Westview Press), 1994.

Coldberg, Andrew C., "Challenges to Post-Cold War Balance of Power," in Kegley, Charles. W., and Wittkopf, Eugene R., (eds.), *The Future of American Foreign Policy* (New York: St. Martin's Press), 1992.

Corbridge, Stuart Corbridge, "Maximizing Entropy? New Geopolitical Orders and the Internationalizing of Business," in Demko and Wood, *Reordering the World.*

Dannreuther, Roland, "Russia, Central Asia and the Persian Gulf," *Survival,* Number 4, 1993.

DeSantis, Hugh, "Europe and Asia Without America," *World Policy Journal,* Autumn 1993.

Doyle, Michael W., *"Liberalism and World Politics Revisited,"* in Charles W. Kegley (ed.), *Controversies in International Relations Theory: Realism and Neoliberal Challenge* (New York: St. Martin's Press), 1995.

van Evera, Stephen, "Primed for Peace: Europe After the Cold War," *International Security*, Number 3, 1990.

Fairbanks, Charles H., Jr., "A Tired Anarchy," *The National Interest*, Spring 1995.

Friedman, Edward, "A Failed Chinese Modernity," *Daedalus*, Spring 1993.

--------, "China's North-South Split and the Forces of Disintegration," *Current History*, September 1993

Fukuyama, Francis, "The End of History," *The National Interest*, Summer 1989.

Funabashi, Yoichi, "The Asianization of Asia," *Foreign Affairs*, November/December 1993.

Gaddis, John Lewis, "International Relations Theory and the End of the Cold War," *International Security*, Number 3, 1993.

--------, "The Long Peace," *International Security*, Number 4, 1986.

Gerace, Michael P., "Transforming the Pattern of Conflict: Geopolitics and Post-Cold War Europe," *Comparative Strategy*, Volume 11, 1992.

Gibney, Frank, "Creating a Pacific Community," *Foreign Affairs*, November/December 1993.

Gilpin, Robert G., "The Richness of the Tradition of Political Realism," in Keohane, (ed.), *Neorealism and Its Critics* (New York: Columbia University Press), 1986.

Haggard, Stephan, and Simmons, Beth A., "Theories of International Regimes," *International Organization*, Summer 1987.

Hamm, Bernd, "Europe: A Challenge to the Social Sciences," in Kazancigill, Ali, (ed.), *Europe in the Making* (Southampton: Blackwell Publishers/UNESCO), 1992.

Hassner, Pierre, "Europe and the Contradictions in American Policy," in Rosecrance, Richard, (ed.), *America as an Ordinary Power* (Ithaca, NY: Cornell University Press), 1976.

Hobden, Stephen, "Geopolitical Space or Civilization? The International System in the Work of Michael Mann," *International Relations*, Number 6, December 1995.

Hoffman, Stanley, "Delusions of World Order," *New York Review of Books*, April 9, 1992.

House, Karen Elliott, "Who Will Manage the Next Superpower?" *The Wall Street Journal,* November 26, 1996.

Hudson, Michael C., "After the Gulf War: Prospects for Democratization in the Arab World", *Middle East Journal,* Number 3, 1991.

Huntington, Samuel, "The Clash of Civilizations," *Moscow News,* February 3-9, 1995.

Ikenberry, John G., "Rethinking the Origins of American Hegemony," *Political Science Quarterly,* Fall 1989.

--------, "Salvaging the G7," *Foreign Affairs,* Spring 1993.

Jervis, Robert, "From Balance to Concert: A Study of International Security Cooperation", *World Politics,* October 1985.

Kahler, Miles, "A World of Blocs," *World Policy Journal,* Spring 1995.

Kearns, Gerry, "Fin-de-Siècle Geopolitics: Mackinder, Hobson and Theories of Global Closure," Taylor, Peter J., (ed.), *Political Geography of the Twentieth Century* (London: Belhaven Press), 1993.

Kegley, Charles W., Jr., "Does the US Have a Role in the Future European Security System?" in Cuthbertson, Ian M., (ed.), *Redefining the CSCE* (New York and Helsinki: Institute for EastWest Studies and Finnish Institute of International Affairs), 1992.

--------, "Explaining Great-Power Peace: The Sources of Prolonged Postwar Stability", in Kegley, (ed.), *The Long Postwar Peace* (New York: Harper-Collins), 1991.

Keohane, Robert O., and Hoffman, Stanley, "Institutional Change in Europe in the 1980s," in Keohane and Hoffman, (eds.), *The New European Community: Decision Making and Institutional Change* (Boulder: Westview Press), 1991.

Keohane, Robert O., and Martin, Lisa L., "The Promise of Institutionalist Theory," *International Security,* Summer 1993.

Kissinger, Henry A., "Balance of Power Sustained," in Allison, Graham, and Treverton, Gregory, (eds.), *Rethinking America's Security: Beyond Cold War to New World Order* (New York: Norton), 1992.

Klare, Michael T., "The Next Great Arms Race," *Foreign Affairs,* Volume 72, 1993.

Kristof, Nicholas D., "The Rise of China," *Foreign Affairs,* November/December 1993.

Krugman, Paul, "The Myth of Asia's Miracle," *Foreign Affairs,* November/December 1994.

Kupchan, Charles A., and Kupchan, Clifford A., "The Promise of Collective Security," *International Security,* Summer 1993.

Lake, David A., "Powerful Pacifists: Democratic States and War," *American Political Science Review,* March 1992.

Lal, Deepak, "Trade Blocs and Multipolar Free Trade," *Journal of Common Market Studies,* Number 3, 1993.

Layne, Christopher, "The Unipolar Illusion," *International Security,* Volume 17, 1993.

Lennon, Alexander T., "Trading Guns, Not Butter," *China Business Review,* March 1994.

Levy, Jack S., "The Causes of War: A Review of Theories and Evidence," in Tetlock, Philip E., et al (eds.), *Behavior, Society and Nuclear War* (New York: Oxford University Press).

----------, "Polarity of the System and International Stability: An Empirical Analysis," in Sabrosky, Alan Ned, (ed.), *Polarity and War* (Boulder, CO: Westview Press), 1985.

Lieven, Anatol, "A New Iron Curtain," *The Atlantic Monthly,* January 1996.

Lind, Michael, "Pax Atlantica: The Case for Euramerica," *World Policy Journal,* Number 1, 1996.

Lucas, Michael R., *The Clinton Administration and the Search for a Multilateral Economic Policy: The Role of GATT, NAFTA and APEC* (unpublished manuscript: 1993).

Luttwak, Edward, "From Geopolitics to Geo-economics," *The National Interest,* Summer 1990.

MacFarlane, S. Neil, and Weiss, Thomas. G., "Regional Organizations and Regional Security," *Security Studies,* Autumn 1992.

MacNeill, Jim, "Ecogeopolitics After Rio," in Hans d'Orville (ed.), *Perspectives of Global Responsibility* (New York: InterAction Council), 1993.

Manning, Robert A., "The Asian Paradox: Toward a New Architecture," *World Policy Journal,* Summer 1993.

Mastel, Greg, "A New U.S. Trade Policy Toward China," *The Washington Quarterly,* Winter 1996.

Matlock, Jack F., Jr., "The Struggle for the Kremlin," *New York Review of Books,* August 8, 1996.

Maynes, Charles William, "Bottom-Up Foreign Policy," *Foreign Policy,* Autumn 1996.

Mead, Walter Russell, "On the Road to Ruin: Winning the Cold War, Losing Economic Peace," *Harpers,* March 1990.

Mearsheimer, John J., "Back to the Future: Instability in Europe After the Cold War," *International Security,* Summer 1990.

--------, "The False Promise of International Institutions," *International Security,* Winter 1994/95.

--------, "A Realist Reply," *International Security,* Summer 1993.

Nathan, Andrew J., "Beijing Blues," *The New Republic,* January 23, 1995.

Nelson, Daniel N., *"Great Powers and World Peace,"* in Klare, Michael T., and Thomas, Daniel C., (eds.), *World Security: Challenges for a New Century* (New York: St. Martin's Press), 1993.

Norton, August Richard, "The Future of Civil Society in the Middle East," *Middle East Journal,* Number 2, 1993.

Nye, Joseph, "American Strategy After Bipolarity," *International Affairs,* Number 3, 1990.

--------, and Owens, Wiliam A., "America's Information Age," *Foreign Affairs,* March/April 1996.

Odell, Peter R., "International Oil: A Return to U.S. Hegemony," *World Today,* November 1994.

Paarlberg, Robert L., "Rice Bowls and Dust Bowls," *Foreign Affairs,* May/June 1996.

Parker, Geoffrey, "Political Geography and Geopolitics" in Parker (ed.), *Contemporary International Relations: A Guide to Theory* (London: Pinter Publishers), 1994.

Pelz, Stephen, "Changing International Systems, The World Balance of Power, and the United States: 1776-1976," *Diplomatic History,* Winter 1991.

Petrella, Riccardo, "A Global Agora vs. Gated City-Republics," *New Perspectives Quarterly,* Winter 1995.

Ruggie, John Gerard, "The False Promise of Realism," *International Security,* Summer 1993.

Rusi, Alpo, "Regional Stability in the Post-Cold War Era," in *Yearbook of Finnish Foreign Policy* (Helsinki: Finnish Institute of International Affairs), 1991.

--------, "Is This the Chance for a New Euro-Atlantic Alliance?" in Cuthbertson, Ian M., (ed.), *Redefining the CSCE* (New York and Helsinki: Institute for EastWest Studies and Finnish Institute of International Affairs), 1992.

Safty, Adel, "The Arab-Israeli Balance of Power After the Storm," *International Relations,* December 1994.

Sakakibara, Eisuke, "The End of Progressivism--A Search for New Goals," *Foreign Affairs,* September/October 1995.

Salomon, Richard H., *"Who Will Shape the Emerging Structure of East Asia?"* in Mandelbaum (ed.), *The Strategic Quadrangle in East Asia.*

Schmidt, Helmut, "Die nahe Zukunft: der Ferne Osten," *Die Zeit,* November 26, 1993.

Schweller, Randall L., "Domestic Structure and Preventive War," *World Politics*, January 1992.

Segal, Gerald, "The Coming Confrontation Between China and Japan?" *World Policy Journal,* Summer 1993.

Smil, Vaclav, "How Rich is China?" *Current History,* September 1993.

Snyder, Jack, "Averting Anarchy in the New Europe", *International Security,* Number 4, 1990.

--------, "The New Nationalism: Realist Interpretations and Beyond," in Rosecrance, Richard, and Stein, Anthony A., (eds.), *The Domestic Bases of Grand Strategy* (Ithaca, NY: Cornell University Press), 1993.

Starr, S. Frederick, "Making Eurasia Stable," *Foreign Affairs,* January/February 1996.

Taylor, Peter J., *"Geopolitical World Orders,"* in Taylor, (ed.), *Political Geography of the Twentieth Century: A Global Analysis*, 1993.

Toffler, Alvin, and Toffler, Heidi, "Mapping out a Trisected World," *International Herald Tribune.*

Volten, Peter M.E., "Power Politics or International Organi zation in Central and Eastern Europe," in de Wilde, Jaap, and Wiberg, Hakan, (eds.), *Organized Anarchy in Europe: The Role of States and Intergovernmental Organizations* (London: I.B. Tauris), 1996.

Wagner, Harrison R., "The Theory of Games and the Balance of Power," *World Politics*, July 1986.

Wendt, Alexander, "Anarchy is What States Make of It: The Social Construction of Power Politics," *International Relations*, Spring 1992.

--------, "Collective Identity Formation and the International States," *American Political Science Review*, June 1994.

--------, "Constructing International Politics," *International Security*, Summer 1993.

Zakaria, Fareed, "Is Realism Finished?", *The National Interest*, Winter 1992/ 93.

Zolberg, Aristide R., "Origins of the Modern World System: A Missing Link," *World Politics*, 1981.

Periodicals and Miscellany

The Economist
The International Herald Tribune
Moscow News
The New York Times
Nikkei Weekly
Trud
The Wall Street Journal
Statistics of Finland

Commission of the European Union, *"Communication from the Commission: A Long-Term Policy for China-Europe Relations,"* (COM[95] 279 final; July, 1995).

---------, *"Reinforcing Political Union and Preparing for Enlargement,"* Opinion on Intergovernmental Conference 1996 (manuscript completed in February 1996).

Friis, Lykke, *"A Look into the Crystal Ball: Scenarios for Eastern Enlargement,"* prepared for the International Political Science Association seminar on "The European Parliament, the Commission, and the Intergovernmental Conference of 1996," Brussels, July 3-5, 1996.

Holsti, Kalevi J.i, *"A 'Zone of Civility' in European Diplomatic Relations? The CSCE and Conflict Resolution,"* (Paper presented at the annual meeting of the International Studies Association, Atlanta, GA, March/April 1992).

Malaska, Pentti, *"Progress, Nature, Technology,"* WFSF XIII World Conference Paper, Turku (Finland), August 28, 1993.

Montes, Manuel F., *"Long-Term Projections for China and India,"* a paper prepared at Wider/UNU Institute, Helsinki, December 6, 1996.

Popov, Vladimir, *"Is Russia Likely to 'Saddle' Economic Growth?"* a paper prepared at the Wider/UNU Institute, Helsinki, December 1996.

Rahr, Alexander, and Krause, Joachim, *"Russia's New Foreign Policy,"* a study undertaken for the European Commission (Bonn: Research Institute of the German Society for Foreign Affairs), May 15, 1995.

Rutanen, Pasi, *"The Tripolar World: The Dangers of Fragmentation and the Role of the OECD,"* World Affairs Council of San Antonio (Texas), January 13, 1994.

Weidenfeld, Werner, and Janning, Josef, *"The New Europe: Strategies for Differential Integration,"* paper presented at the International Bertelsmann Forum, January 19-20, 1996.

"A Report of the Independent Working Group on the Future of the United Nations," (Yale University and the Ford Foundation; June 19, 1995).

About the Book and Author

Examining the international system from a geopolitical and geoeconomic perspective, Alpo Rusi provides a broad vision and bold forecast of the emerging strategic landscape for the coming century. An asymmetrical world system is emerging. The United States is now the sole true world power; it forms the core of a unipolar order characterized by an uneven division of world power and economic resources. Rusi argues, however, that this post–Cold War "order" will not survive into the next century.

Rusi suggests that the power vacuum in the former Soviet empire will be filled by China in Asia and by the European Union in Eastern Europe, Russia's disintegration and decline in world power status will continue but may have reached its bottom line economically, and Islam will gain strength in various parts of the world, embracing a new international role. He also predicts that the world will be split into four or five distinct trading blocs: A European bloc formed around the European Union; an East Asian bloc, potentially strong, interventionist, and even aggressive, formed around China and the Singapore economic region; Japan, as a strong and still competitive economic power; and a Pan-American bloc, also strong but potentially isolationist, formed around the United States. One of the question marks will be the future ability of an orthodox Russia to facilitate conditions for an economic space.

According to Rusi, these trading blocs will develop new political or geopolitical interests. For example, the European bloc will extract fossil fuels from the former Soviet Union instead of the Middle East, thereby changing partly the existing global trade system. Each bloc will have certain internal problems—the Europeans will be linked to the unstable successors to the Soviet Union, the East Asian bloc will have to contemplate whether China's economic growth and geopolitical expansions will create a new bipolar world in the early twenty-first century, and the Pan-American bloc will struggle with continuing political and economic instability in South and Central America.

Finally, Rusi warns that it is crucial for the European and Pan-American blocs to build upon the traditional Euro-Atlantic relationship. Without it, he argues, a truly polarized—and potentially hostile—bloc system could take root, most likely lining the "Western pan-regions" against China's expansiveness.

Alpo M. Rusi is currently Foreign Policy Advisor to the president of Finland, Deputy Chief of the Cabinet, and visiting associate professor at Helsinki University. In addition to his diplomatic duties, he has written several books, including *After the Cold War: Europe's New Political Architecture.*

Index